THE
FEDERAL
CONVENTION
OF 1787

North Carolina
In The Great Crisis

By
BURTON CRAIGE
Of the Winston-Salem and Salisbury Bars

Printed by
Expert Graphics
Richmond, Virginia

Contents

Illustrations

BURTON CRAIGE
1875-1945

About the Author

BURTON CRAIGE
1875-1945

Born in Salisbury, North Carolina, and educated at the University of North Carolina where he graduated in 1897 with highest honors, being president of Phi Beta Kappa. He was admitted to the Bar in 1901 and joined his father and brother in the practice of law in Salisbury. He served in the state legislature and later moved to Winston-Salem to become general counsel for the Reynolds Tobacco Company.

He married Jane Henderson Boyden of Salisbury in 1911, and they were the parents of two sons and a daughter. In 1917 he rejoined his old partnership with offices in Salisbury and Winston-Salem, and continued the private practice with his brother, nephews and son.

Various public honors were bestowed upon him, carrying with them larger responsibilities. Governor O. Max Gardner appointed him to the North Carolina Constitutional Revision Commission in 1932 and unquestionably this duty stimulated his study of constitutional law, which brought forth this book. He served as chairman of the Winston-Salem Committee to celebrate the 150th anniversary of the federal Constitution. He was the author of various biographical sketches and memoirs.

He was a trustee of Salem College and the University of North Carolina for many years where he endowed a professorship of jurisprudence. In 1937 the University bestowed upon him an honorary degree of Doctor of Laws. His life-long devotion to North Carolina remained unbounded. This was matched by the respect and admiration of his contemporaries. He died leaving this book in manuscript form.

It was my father's intention to distribute a copy to each of the high schools in the state, to the various public libraries, and to institutions of higher learning. This is being accomplished with the approval and assistance of the North Carolina Commission on the Bicentennial of the United States Constitution and with the aid of N.C. Department of Public Instruction.

Its publication wishes to recognize the helpful critiques of the late Professors A. R. Newsome and Hugh Lefler of the Department of History at the University of North Carolina; the late Mr. James S. Brawley of Salisbury; Miss Carolyn L. Teacher of Winston-Salem; Ms. Anne Morrison of the U.S. Commission of the Constitutional Bicentennial; and Dr. Rob Sikorski of the staff of the North Carolina Commission on the Bicentennial of the United States Constitution, and to Superintendent Craig Phillips and Dr. John Ellington of the North Carolina Department of Public Instruction.

Archibald Craige
Keswick, Virginia

On the following page is a copy of the famous painting by Howard Chandler Christy commissioned by the United States Congress in 1939. It measures 20 by 30 feet, and now hangs in our Nation's Capitol.

Mr. Christy spent five years of research and study on the subject. An effort was made to include all of the delegates as they assembled in Independence Hall in Philadelphia on the final day of meeting, September 17, 1787.

The delegates wore their best clothes on that memorable day. Richard Dobbs Spaight of North Carolina appears to be affixing his signature to the famous document just in front of President Washington. Standing near him are his fellow delegates William Blount and Hugh Williamson.

Scene at the Signing of the Constitution of the United States

Scene at the Signing of the Constitution of the United States

1. Washington, George . . . . Va.
2. Franklin, Benjamin . . . . Pa.
3. Madison, James . . . . Va.
4. Hamilton, Alexander. . . . . N.Y.
5. Morris, Gouverneur . . . . Pa.
6. Morris, Robert. . . . . Pa.
7. Wilson, James. . . . . Pa.
8. Pinckney, Chas. Cotesworth . . . S.C.
9. Pinckney, Chas. . . . . S.C.
10. Rutledge, John . . . . S.C.
11. Butler, Pierce. . . . . S.C.
12. Sherman, Roger. . . . . Conn.
13. Johnson, William Samuel. . . . . . Conn.

14. McHenry, James . . . . Md.
15. Read, George . . . . Del.
16. Bassett, Richard . . . . Del.
17. Spaight, Richard Dobbs . . . . N.C.
18. Blount, William . . . . N.C.
19. Williamson, Hugh . . . . N.C.
20. Jenifer, Daniel of St. Thomas . . . Md.
21. King, Rufus . . . . Mass.
22. Gorham, Nathaniel . . . . Mass.
23. Dayton, Jonathan . . . . N.J.
24. Carroll, Daniel. . . . . Md.
25. Few, William. . . . . Ga.
26. Baldwin, Abraham . . . . Ga.

27. Langdon, John . . . . N.H.
28. Gilman, Nicholas. . . . . N.J.
29. Livingston, William . . . . N.J.
30. Paterson, William . . . . N.J.
31. Mifflin, Thomas . . . . Pa.
32. Clymer, Goerge . . . . Pa.
33. FitzSimons, Thomas . . . . Pa.
34. Ingersoll, Jared . . . . Pa.
35. Bedford, Gunning, Jr. . . . . Del.
36. Broom, Jacob. . . . . Del.
37. Dickinson, John. . . . . Del.
38. Blair, John . . . . Va.
39. Brearley, David . . . . N.J.
40. Jackson, William (Secretary)

FOREWORD

These articles in part were published in the Winston-Salem Journal and Salisbury Morning Herald, in 1937 during the celebration of the one hundred and fiftieth birthday of the formation of the Federal Constitution. Since then, they have been revised. Therefore it becomes advisable to put them in more permanent form.

There is no claim to originality in the writings. "The thing that hath been, it is that which shall be; and that which is done is that which shall be done: and there is no new thing under the sun."[1] Here has been gathered the fruit of other men's labor. The only tie that binds is the author's share in the work, but it is hoped that young North Carolinians will be stimulated to investigate the part taken by their State in forming our fundamental law.

There was great confusion in our national government during the years immediately preceding the adoption of our Federal Constitution. On July 12, 1776, a few days after the Declaration of Independence had been signed, Articles of Confederation and Perpetual Union were reported in the Continental Congress. The Congress could not agree on a form for submission to the states until November 17, 1777. They were not finally passed and ratified by all of the states until March 1, 1781, when Maryland became sufficiently assured that the vast territorial possessions of some of her sister states would be ceded to the United States and entered her name to the Articles. By that time, the Revolutionary War was about over. Under the Articles nine states, usually, were sufficient to complete congressional action; but even then a belligerent state was beyond control. This will give a preliminary background to the difficulties confronting the disputing states in their efforts to form a Union.

Even before this time the colonies had attempted to form some sort of a joint association, at the Albany Congress of 1754, instigated by the mother country, and at the so-called unconstitutional gathering of the Stamp Act Congress of 1765 in New York. The Continental Congress began its session on September 5, 1774, and there were at that time inter-colonial committees of correspondence. But these Articles of Confederation and Perpetual Union comprised the first charter under which the states attempted anything like joint action. John Adams, writing to his wife on July 29, said: "If a confederation should take place, one great question is, how we shall vote? Whether each Colony shall count one; or whether each shall have weight in proportion to its numbers, or wealth, or exports and imports, or a compound ration of all."[2]

This was one of the greatest of all of the stumbling blocks in the formation of the union. In the Articles of Confederation each state was given an equal vote, regardless of its wealth, its size, or its importance. The pressing necessities of war doubtless forced this equal voting strength, for which each of the small states contended with the threat that none of them would enter a confederation on any other terms. Some of the larger states thought that the smaller ones were exercising authority out of all proportion to their real importance.

The Articles of Confederation contained many defects. Some of the defects in the plan were recapitulated by a distinguished Philadelphia contemporary, Pelatiah Webster, as follows:

"But on trial of it in practice, it was found to be extremely weak, defective, totally inefficient, and altogether inadequate to its great ends and purposes. For,

1. It blended the legislative and executive power together in one body.
2. This body, viz, Congress, consisted of but one house, without any check upon their resolutions.
3. The powers of Congress in very few instances were definitive and final; in the most important articles of government they could do no more than recommend

to the several States, the consent of every one of
which was necessary to give legal sanction to any act
so recommended.
4. They could assess and levy no taxes.
5. They could institute and execute no punishments,
except in the military department.
6. They had no power of deciding or controlling the
contentions and disputes of different States with
each other.
7. They could not regulate the general trade; or,
8. Even make laws to secure either public treaties with
foreign countries, or the persons of public ambassa-
dors, or to punish violations or injuries done to
either of them.
9. They could institute no general judiciary powers.
10. They could regulate no public road, canals, or inland
navigation, etc., etc., etc."3

The states stumbled through the Revolutionary War under the
Articles of Confederation; but it was realized by some of the more
important leaders that something had to be done, if a union was to
exist.

A principal trouble was the jealousy of each of the several states
over its freedom, sovereignty, and independence. In the Definitive Treaty of Peace between the mother country and her former
colonies, concluded September 3rd, 1783, George III, King of
England and Ireland, declared the Colonies to be free, sovereign,
and independent states, with no distinction or classification as to
the importance of any one of them. It was a task for the states to
forget or to forego the importance of this high-sounding language,
so generously conceded by the King, following the hard fought
battles of the Revolution.

Even after the Articles of Confederation were adopted, the
commercial conflicts between the states continued to be exceed-
ingly annoying. New York, for instance, collected impost duties

on imported foreign goods and passed them on to her sister states. New Jersey, between Philadelphia and New York, had no recourse but to pay the duties which her position entailed. She was likened to "a cask tapped at both ends". North Carolina, with Charleston on the South and the Virginia harbors on the North, was described as "a stump bleeding at both ends".

Maryland had claims upon the Potomac and upon Chesapeake Bay; but Virginia controlled the capes at the outlet. Delaware Bay and River provided fighting ground between Pennsylvania, New Jersey, and Delaware. This is just a partial insight into some of the causes of the conflicts between the states. In the North Carolina Convention at Hillsboro, Col. William Richardson Davie graphically expressed the fight between the states when he said that "encroachments of some States on the rights of others and of all on those of the Confederation are incontestable proofs of the weakness and imperfection of that system".

One serious trouble was caused by the fact that England was largely in control of foreign commerce. New York knew that any displeasure with England, if brought to an issue, would result in her loss of British trade. England constantly threatened to make arrangements with some sister state anxious for trade and for the control of the impost duties, which New York and a few others collected and passed on to sister states, doubtless with such enlargement as the traffic would bear. James Madison said that Robert Yates and John Lansing, the New York delegates to the Constitution Convention, had left it because their party in New York was fearful of losing the commercial advantages of taxing the consumption of her neighbors with her impost duties. New York refused even to grant a duty of five per cent on imposts, to which other states were willing due to the urgent needs caused by the Revolution. New York foresaw the movement on foot to transfer the regulation of commerce from the states to a central authority. North Carolina favored the central government as the collector of imposts.[4]

The Mount Vernon Compact of March 1785 between Virginia and Maryland resulted in some local peace as regards trade on the Potomac; but it was hoped that enlargement of the compromise could be had by a convention which was recommended by the Mount Vernon Commissioners. This general trade convention met with favor and nine of the states appointed commissioners to meet at Annapolis the first Monday in September, 1786.

The enthusiasm of North Carolina for this Annapolis Convention has been overlooked almost entirely. It is generally reported that North Carolina failed to attend, which is only a partial truth and unfair to the State. She did more than has since been recorded. Governor Caswell, on the advice of the Council, appointed former Governor Abner Nash, Alfred Moore, Dr. Hugh Williamson, John Gray Blount, and Philemon Hawkins as commissioners to the Convention.[5] Governor Caswell wrote to Honorable Edmund Randolph of Virginia, to Governor Patrick Henry of Virginia, to Honorable Charles Biddle of Pennsylvania, to Governor James Bowdoin of Massachusetts, to Governor Van Dyke of Delaware and doubtless others telling them of the appointment of the North Carolina Commissioners.[6] He also sent to John Gray Blount, one of the State's largest shippers and importers, the resolutions of Virginia, Massachusetts, and Pennsylvania.[7] All of these acts evidence North Carolina's interest and preparation for the Convention. Dr. Williamson accepted the appointment, "from a zealous desire to promote the mercantile interests of this State".[8] Williamson then wrote to Governor Caswell that one of Blount's clerk's had reported him so ill of fever that he could not leave on the forth of September, the date they were due at Annapolis. However, Blount said he hoped to leave in a few days. At the same time he advised Williamson to go on, as the information which he had might be useful in the Convention.[9] Dr. Williamson lost some time waiting on Blount, or Governor Nash, who was also ill, as he considered that a single commissioner would have no vote. Arriving in Norfolk on September 7, he encountered one of the customary September storms and did not reach Annpolis until September 14th, the date when the Convention adjourned. Dr. Williamson said the Convention knew that other states were on the road; but that the Commissioners first assembled had given "sufficient reason" for not sitting longer. Had the Convention proceeded to business, instead of adjourning, he said that he would have been on time.[10] Inability to call the Constitutional Convention, as far as this fragmentary gathering was concerned, was certainly "sufficient reason" for not sitting longer; but it was no reason for historians ever after ignoring North Carolina's earnest interest and her serious endeavor to participate in this commercial conclave which brought about the Philadelphia Convention.

A letter from John Dickinson of Delaware, as chairman, together with the Report of the Commissioners of the Annapolis Convention, came before the Continental Congress during its session on February 21, 1787, as the order of the day. This report was referred to a Grand Committee of which William Blount of North Carolina was a member. It may be interesting to state that this Annapolis report made mention of the fact that North Carolina had appointed Commissioners to the Annapolis Convention. The Grand Committee's report was embodied in a resolution "entirely coinciding" with the report of the Annapolis Commissioners, as to the "inefficiency of the Federal Government" and "the necessity of devising such further provisions as shall render the same adequate to the exigencies of the Union," and "strongly recommending to the different legislatures of the several States to send forward delegates to meet at the proposed convention to be held on the second Monday of May next at the city of Philadelphia."[11] The time of meeting in Philadelphia, as suggested in the Annapolis report, was never changed.

The New York delegation moved a postponement of the report of the Grand Committee to give opportunity to consider instructions from their constituents. On the "yeas" and "nays" the motion was lost, with New Jersey, Pennsylvania, North Carolina and South Carolina opposing the motion, and Massachusetts, New York, and Virginia favoring the New York motion to postpone. Connecticut and Georgia were divided, and Delaware and Maryland were absent.

Thereupon the delegates from Massachusetts determined to take charge of the proceedings and to restrict the Convention to the "sole and express purpose of revising the Articles of Confederation and reporting to Congress, etc." The words "sole and express purpose of revising" were not in the report of the Annapolis Commissioners nor in the resolution of the Grand Committee of the Continental Congress. This proposition "solely to revise the articles" caused one of the real disputes in the Constitutional Convention because it was contended that the Convention's authority was thus limited. The Massachusetts resolution was adopted on Wednesday, February 21, 1787.[12] The Philadelphia Convention assembled in due course and subsequently framed our Constitution, being little influenced by the sole authority to revise the Articles of Confederation and Perpetual Union.

Chapter 1

THE CONVENTION
North Carolina in the Great Crisis
The Federal Convention of 1787, at Philadelphia

Before North Carolina was notified formally of the February 21 call by the Continental Congress for a Convention of the States to be held on the second Monday in May 1787, at Philadelphia, "for the sole and express purpose of revising the Articles of Confederation," the General Assembly of North Carolina elected delegates to it on January 6, 1787. It was then enacted "That five commissioners be appointed by joint ballot of both House of Assembly, ... authorized as deputies, .. to meet and confer with such deputies as may be appointed by the other States ... and to discuss and decide upon the most effectual means to remove the defects of our federal union and to procure the enlarged purposes which it was intended to effect, etc." The powers of the North Carolina deputies were somewhat broader than the purposes set forth in the Congressional call. The Assembly evidently sensed the necessity for doing more than merely revising the ineffectual Articles of Confederation, as ultimately was done, though not without a fight.[1] The Governor was authorized to supply vacancies. This General Assembly elected Richard Caswell, Alexander Martin, William Richardson Davie, Richard Dobbs Spaight and Willie Jones as deputies.[2] Willie Jones, "rich and colorful leader of Jeffersonian Democracy in North Carolina", declined his appointment. On April 3, 1787, Dr. Hugh Williamson was appointed to succeed Jones.

Governor Caswell resigned without serving and on April 23, 1787, appointed William Blount in his stead.[3] All five of the deputies, or delegates, attended the Convention; but William

Blount, Hugh Williamson, and Richard Dobbs Spaight were the only North Carolina delegates who were present at the close of the Convention and who signed the Constitution for North Carolina.[4] The members of the Federal Convention from the several states were variously designated as commissioners, or as deputies, or as delegates; but the most usual designation of them has been as delegates.

The record of North Carolina compares favorably with the records of the other states. In all there were sixty-five delegates—some say seventy-three were elected—only fifty-five of whom attended the Convention.[5] Sixteen of these fifty-five failed, possibly on account of disagreement with it, to sign the Constitution. Edmund Randolph, the sponsor of the Virginia Plan, under which the Convention proceeded with its work; George Mason, the author of the Virginia Bill of Rights; Luther Martin of Maryland; and Elbridge Gerry, of Massachusetts, the chairman of the Grand Committee on representation, were among those who refused to sign. Only three of the seven elected delegates from Virginia, two attending delegates from New Hampshire, two of the four attending from Massachusetts, one of the three elected from New York, four of the five attending from New Jersey, three of the five elected from Maryland, three of the five from North Carolina, and two of the four attending from Georgia signed the Constitution for their respective States.[6]

There was considerable suspicion and diffidence before the Convention assembled and much conflict after it got under way. The little State of Rhode Island and Providence Plantations, jealous of her state sovereignty and fearful of losing the equal voting strength which she was enjoying with other states under the Articles of Confederation, appointed no delegates. Rhode Island sensed the real purpose of the convention though the call for it was drafted in guarded language. It was feared by her, with reason, that the Articles of Confederation, fairly satisfactory to the small states because of the equal voting power ensured them, would be supplanted by a system more favorable to the large states. Delaware expressly instructed her delegates not to agree to any change in her equal voting power under the Confederation.[7] The delegates from New Hampshire, another small state, were particular not to arrive until after the great crisis over voting power had been settled.

All of the North Carolina delegates, except one, were educated in the best colleges and universities of this country and Europe. Of the eight delegates from all States who were educated abroad, two of them, Williamson and Spaight, were from North Carolina. Governor Spaight attended the University of Glasgow. Dr. Williamson was graduated in the first class of the University of Pennsylvania, attended three foreign Universities, and was honored with an LL. D. degree by the University of Leyden. He was one of the most scholarly members of the Philadelphia Convention. North Carolina had as large a proportion of college-bred gentlemen among the attending delegates as any other state except New Jersey, all of whose attending delegates were college men.

Of the New Jersey delegation, however, William Churchill Houston, "the fighting pedagogue," was a native of Cabarrus County, North Carolina. He graduated from Princeton with the Class of 1768 and became Professor of Mathematics and Natural Philosophy, in which capacity he received the praise of James Madison, one of his pupils. He was, with the exception of Dr. Witherspoon, the only full Princeton professor at the outbreak of the Revolution. He married Jane Dickinson, the granddaughter of the first president, served as a captain in the army, was a member of the Continental Congress, as well as other legislative bodies; was elected comptroller of the treasury; became an eminent lawyer; served as a member of the Annapolis Convention; and, among other honors, according to the Princeton account, was, on November 23, 1786, chosen chairman of the New Jersey delegation to the Philadelphia Convention. He died August 12, 1788, on his way to pay a visit to his old home in North Carolina.[8]

The North Carolina's delegates had traveled extensively and had overcome provincialism by contact with the outside world. All of them had some knowledge of cities and men. All of them had performed patriotic services in local or continental legislative halls. All of them had served in some capacity in the field in the cause of liberty, and all who signed the Constitution had served in the Continental Congress. They were well informed from personal experience on public affairs prior and subsequent to the American Revolution.

It is refreshing to feel that the North Carolina delegates were, to some extent, grounded in the humanities. They must have felt that it was worthwhile to think as well as to act and to educate the heart as well as the head. They knew that power could be improved by the addition of a little wisdom. They certainly showed in the great crisis that they could put aside self-interest and give some attention, as Thomas Jefferson expressed it in the Declaration of Independence, to "a decent respect to the opinions of mankind" that truth might prevail and power might be curbed.

Of course, economic conditions played a large part in the framing of the Federal Constitution; but North Carolina was situated a little differently from some of her sister states in this particular, and her delegates were not so much influenced by these considerations, as were some others. While North Carolina had considerable commercial and shipping interests, she could not compare with the states that had larger and better port facilities, like Massachusetts, Virginia, and South Carolina. While she had a number of slaveholders she did not have as many large slaveholding planters as either the James River section of Virginia or the Charleston section of South Carolina. While she may have been less important than Virginia or South Carolina, when measured by her nabob planters, she doubtless had a larger proportion of small well-to-do farmers especially in her western areas than either of these states. there was not in her borders such a wide cleavage between the moneyed and the unmoneyed populations, as was evidenced in some of her sister states. In her bounds there were large settlements of Scotch-Irish and Germans who, like the old Scot, Judge James Wilson, in the Constitutional Convention, thought that property rights were not the only consideration; but that "the cultivation and improvement of the human mind was the most noble object" of government. North Carolina had some holders of public securities; but these papers were mostly bought up by northern speculators as stated by Charles A. Beard in his *Economic Interpretation of the Constitution.* This powerful group of speculators had little influence on the North Carolina delegation, which was a fair cross section of the better population of the State and was representative of her mercantile, manufacturing, land holders, professional, commercial, shipping, and other groups.

The small farmers, mechanics, and debtor groups were not personally represented nor was the German element. There was no member of the delegation who could be classed as a Gracchi Leveler mad about the unequal distribution of property. The North Carolina delegates were well-to-do and conservative in the main, independent like their State, and favorable to a stable government of law and order. Most of them leaned toward the federalist way of thinking, though the State was at first largely anti-federal, especially in the western sections. The west was not, as such, represented on the delegation, unless Governor Alexander Martin be so considered. Governor Martin was a large land owner, successful planter, and man of affairs, like many in the Albemarle and Brunswick sections, as was also Colonel Davie who moved from Salisbury to Halifax after the Revolution. Governor Martin was a little different from the Scotch Irish with whom he grew up, though there were many of them who were well-to-do in land and slaves, and strongly federalistic in the areas around Salisbury and Charlotte. There were many who disagreed with him in and around Halifax, which section furnished the chief leader of the opposition to the Federal Constitution in North Carolina, Willie Jones.

North Carolina not only sent a distinguished delegation to the Convention, but she also held an important place among the Original Thirteen. In the 1790 census she was listed as fourth in population although when this census was taken North Carolina no longer included Tennessee. In 1787, the year of the Convention, Tennessee was a part of North Carolina. A separate census was taken for Maine and Tennessee. Georgia, North Carolina, and Virginia were the largest states in the area. North Carolina furnished more troops to the Revolution than New York. When Governor Tryon of North Carolina sought removal to New York he was told by the authorities in England that he already had a more important position.[9] It is difficult to understand why North Carolina was seldom spoken of as one of the large states. The delegates give some reason for it. In a letter to Governor Caswell, on September 18, they told him that the State had never "enabled" its delegates in Congress to prove the size and importance of the State and, accordingly, that they had not been zealous to magnify the number of their constituents, because their quota of the national debt would have been augmented accordingly. They also said that while they were taking so much care to guard themselves against being imposed upon, their northern brethren were not unattentive to their own particular interest.[10]

It cannot be doubted, viewed in any light, that North Carolina has been overlooked. A good illustration is the appearance of a distinguished historian before the annual meeting of the North Carolina Bar Association in 1927, for the principal address.[11] He referred to the Philadelphia Convention of 1787 and called attention to the country's ignorance of Oliver Ellsworth of Connecticut, whose ingenuity, he said, devised a plan for equal representation in the Senate and thus smoothed out the seemingly irreconcilable conflict over the distribution of voting power in the two legislative branches. He overlooked Judge Ellsworth's colleague, Roger Sherman, another great advocate of state rights and the first delegate, or deputy, to introduce the Connecticut compromise before the Convention. It would have been most appropriate if he had referred likewise to the country's ignorance about North Carolina's part in this Convention. "Ellsworth's ingenuity" would have been a mere gesture had not North Carolina made practice out of theory by giving to the Connecticut proposal one of the most important decisive votes ever cast in a law-making assembly. The ratio of representation had been a troublesome question in all of the prior attempts at united action.

In all of these attempts by the colonies and the nascent states, each was treated as an equal unit. In the Stamp Act Congress, for instance, Rhode Island, the smallest colony, had one vote, and Virginia, the most important colony, had one vote. This was the situation after independence in the Continental Congress.[12] As heretofore said, John Adams, on the 29th of July, 1776, when the Articles of Confederation were being considered, wrote his wife about the prime importance of this troublesome question.[13] The exigencies of war forced the larger states to yield to the smaller states and to give them equal strength in the Confederation. This necessary concession became the greatest stumbling block in the Constitutional Convention. The large states thought that equality was preposterous and out of all proportion to the real importance of the small states. The smaller states thought that anything but equality would destroy the independent sovereignty of which they were so jealous and so proud. James Madison, in his notes on the Constitutional Convention, stated that "The great difficulty lies in the affair of representation; and, if this can be adjusted, all others would be surmountable."[14]

The fight between the large and small states over representation all but broke up the Convention. The best evidence that the crisis in the Convention arose out of the fight over the rule of representation in the House and Senate is contained in Article 5 of the Constitution of the United States, which provides that no state, without its consent, shall be deprived of its equal suffrage in the Senate. The small states manfully clung to the last to what they considered essential to their vaunted freedom, sovereignty, and independence and came to terms only when they were assured equality in the Senate. This is the only operative provision in the Federal Constitution that is not subject to amendment in the usual way. It was the aftermath of the great crisis and is a living expression of the compromised in the fight of the small states for their equal suffrage privileges.[14a]

The compromise grew out of a suggestion made by Roger Sherman and Judge Oliver Ellsworth of Connecticut, thus known as the Connecticut Compromise, which provided for equal repre- sentation in the Senate and proportional representation in the House of Representatives. Connecticut theretofore had followed somewhat similar arrangements in her own governmental affairs. This compromise overcame the greatest obstacle before the Convention; but of course there were other defects in the old Articles of Confederation. Some of these defects summarized by a contemporary, have been mentioned.[15]

There was a total absence of the checks and balances to become so prevalent in our Constitution and so conducive to the preserva- tion of the liberty and freedom of the humblest citizen as well as protecting the rights of minorities in a representative democracy. So it may be seen readily that something had to be done, else a general government would be an impossibility. To revise the Articles of Confederation was supposed to be the prime object of the Convention but the leaders realized from the beginning that a mere revision was futile. Upon the meeting of the Convention, it immediately went to work on a new instrument.

It was generally agreed that there must be a distribution of governmental powers among independent legislative, executive, and judicial departments. This had been done in some of the state constitutions which were adopted after the Declaration of Inde- pendence. Just how to exercise these powers under a new instrument was another matter. It was quite a task to forget or to forego any of the high sounding language like "freedom, sovereignty, and independence," so generously bestowed upon each of the colonies by King George in the Definitive Treaty of Peace, after the hard fought battles of the Revolution.[16] Nationally minded delegates like James Madison, James Wilson, Robert Morris, Rufus King, and others, stirred up a hornet's nest as soon as Edmund Randolph's Resolutions, or the Virginia Plan which they supported, was brought before the Convention. These Resolutions provided for proportional representation in both branches of the legislative department. Interesting sidelights showing the trend of events come down to us from such worthies as General George Washington, the presiding officer in the Convention and the nestor of the "secret conclave." He wrote Alexander Hamilton from the Convention that he almost despaired of seeing a favorable issue from the Convention and that he regretted having any interest in the business.[17] He also wrote Thomas Jefferson that the General Government was at an end and that should a remedy not soon be applied, anarchy and confusion would inevitably ensue.[18] Characteristically, he stood like a fortress. He was the one man whom darkest gloom could not completely discourage.

The contribution made by North Carolina and her delegates to our fundamental law will appear from a review of the proceedings of the Convention.

The notes of James Madison on the debates during the Convention constitute the main source of information.[19] Judge Robert Yates of New York also kept notes of the proceedings, until the time that he left the Convention, but they are not so full and comprehensive. There are a few other fragments, like the notes of John Lansing, Jr. Then, too, "Secret Proceedings and Debates" was issued as a Senate Document. This contains, among other information, the speech on the Federal Convention by the Maryland delegate, Luther Martin, before the Maryland Legislature.[20]

The correspondence of the delegates is meagre in detail as they were bound to secrecy. Madison's notes show better than anything how jealous the small states were over their equal voting rights in the two branches of the legislative department of the government and how persistent the large states were for proportional representation in both branches.

Although the Convention was called for the 14th day of May, a quorum did not arrive until the 25th of May. The Randolph Resolves, or the Virginia Plan, which mainly is said to have been the work of James Madison and which provided for proportional representation in both legislative branches was not introduced until the 29th of May. The Convention proceeded with its work on these Resolves.[21] They were referred to the Convention as a Committee of the Whole House, so that there might be more freedom of discussion.[22] The controversy over the rule of suffrage, which raised the greatest dispute in the Convention, began on the 31st day of May and continued, with more or less vehemence until the settlement of the great crisis on the 16th of July. While the Convention was still in Committee of the Whole, David Brearley of New Jersey reminded the delegates that, under the Confederation, states voted equally.[23] Judge William Paterson of New Jersey questioned the power of the Convention to change this voting rule and stated that New Jersey would not confederate on the Virginia Plan, but would rather submit to a monarch or despot.[24] Judge James Wilson of Pennsylvania suggested, that, if the small states would not confederate on the Virginia Plan, Pennsylvania, and perhaps other states, would not confederate on any other.[25]

On June 11th, Roger Sherman of Connecticut suggested the compromise idea of providing for proportional representation in the House and equal state votes in the Senate; but his motion did not receive a second.[26] Sherman then renewed his motion and it was seconded by Judge Oliver Ellsworth of the same state.[27] This became known as the Connecticut Compromise. On a vote on this motion it was lost by six to five, with North Carolina voting against the compromise.[28] North Carolina then voted with five other states for proportional representation in both branches of the legislature.[29] It must be remembered that the Convention, in its deliberations, debated all kinds of unsegregated questions. It is difficult to segregate and assemble the trend of debate of the Great Crisis, or rule of representation.

Before the Virginia Plan was reported back to the Convention from the Committee of the Whole House, postponement was effected in order that small states could be given opportunity to present another plan.[30] Accordingly, on the 15th of June, Judge William Paterson of New Jersey introduced the Paterson Plan, or New Jersey Plan, which was merely a rehash of the Articles of Confederation, with some material changes like the division of governmental powers between legislative, executive, and judicial departments. But it left the federal government in the hands of the states, almost stripped of the necessary federal powers, and retained equal state voting strength in the legislative branch. Judge Paterson suggested that if the Convention wanted to discard the Articles of Confederation, it would be better to return to the states for more power. Judge James Wilson of Pennsylvania, the ablest lawyer in the Convention, countered by stating that he conceived himself authorized to conclude nothing but to propose everything.[31] When the Virginia Plan came before the Convention, after being reported back from the Committee of the Whole House, it passed seven to three, with North Carolina voting in the affirmative.[32]

There was considerable talk about the state governments. On June 25, Dr. Williamson professed himself a friend of such a system as would secure the existence of the state governments. He wanted to know the number of the Senate members and refused to give his vote until he did.[33] He suggested a fixed ratio to the House number but it was not seconded. There followed a long debate, with speeches by James Madison, James Wilson, and Dr.

Williamson on proportional representation and by Roger Sherman and others supporting the principle in the Confederation of equal voting strength.

On June 28 the debate was continued on the seventh Resolution of the Virginia Plan as reported to the Convention from the Committee of the Whole House and John Lansing moved that the word "not" be stricken out so that it might read: "*that* the representation of the first branch be according to the Articles of Confederation."[36] Madison said, "I am against the motion", and so continued at length, with advocates of the large and small states alternately interspersing remarks. At the close of the day, Dr. Franklin remarked: "As a sparrow does not fall without Divine permission, can we suppose that governments can be erected without His will? I move that we have prayers every morning."[37] His motion was seconded by Sherman of Connecticut; but Hamilton objected on the ground that breaking the secrecy of the meeting at this time, with such notice to the public, might cause alarm.

On June 29 it was voted that the rule of representation in the House of Representatives should not follow the Articles of Confederation (equal state vote) but that the first clause of the reported resolution, number seven, should stand as fixed in the Virginia Plan, (proportional representation).[38] This was a six to four vote, with North Carolina as usual lined up with the big states. Then Judge Ellsworth moved that the rule of suffrage in the second branch (Senate) be the same as that established by the Articles of Confederation, viz, that each state have an equal vote.[39]

On the 30th of June the debate became particularly vehement. Judge Wilson again spoke at length on the general principles of representation and the rightful contentions of the large states. Judge Oliver Ellsworth made the sane and quieting remark that the delegates were razing the foundations of the building when they needed only to repair the roof. James Madison, speaking for the big states, remarked that Connecticut least of all should claim adherence to a plighted faith in the Articles of Confederation because she had been lax in the observance of them. And Judge Ellsworth countered that Connecticut if delinquent in raising her quota of war expenses, was so only from inability to perform and that she had plenty of company. He further said that Connecticut had had more men in the field than Virginia. Then followed Colonel Davie of North Carolina, one of the young men of the Convention, with his longest speech. It was calm and conciliatory. He seemed to be of the opinion, according to the notes of James Madison, that the Virginia idea of proportional representation in both legislative branches was impracticable, as it would make the Senate too large a body to possess the activity and qualities required of it. If he were required, said he, to vote on the comparative merits of the report as it stood and the amendment, he would feel constrained to vote for the Connecticut idea; but, he said, equal representation looked like bringing back the old ideas of the Confederation and shutting out all of the advantages expected from a change. Under these conditions he said he could not vote for any plan for the Senate yet proposed. Colonel Davie suggested that there were extremes on both sides, as the proposed union was partly federal and partly national in its character. Chief Justice Robert Yates of New York, who also kept notes on the Convention, reported Colonel Davie as being in favor of the motion of Judge Ellsworth for equality of votes in the Senate.[40] Madison's notes are more complete. Colonel Davie's remarks show that he was for some kind of compromise, for a balance of power between the contending forces. Also Colonel Davie possessed a great deal of independence and, to some extent, was antagonistic to Virginia domination. He insisted upon doing his own thinking. Both he and Dr. Williamson were less influenced by Virginia than most of the Carolinans. Dr. Franklin cited the sensible carpenter who in making a table takes a little from each plank to make a good joint.[42] And so the proceedings, briefly stated, were moving directly along when an explosion all but developed.

After witnessing an adverse vote on a motion to send for New Hampshire, with North Carolina voting against the motion, and several more long talks by "Big State" delegates, the patience of the small states approached exhaustion.[43] Heated remarks from them soon filled the halls. Judge Paterson of New Jersey, one of the most implacable enemies of the Virginia Plan, had said on June 9 that a confederacy supposes sovereignty in the members composing it and sovereignty supposes equality. "Let them unite if they please, but let them remember that they have no authority to compel the others to unit. New Jersey will never confederate on the plan before the Committee. She would be swallowed up." He said that he would not only oppose the plan in the Convention but that on his return home do everything in his power to arouse opposition.[44] Jonathan Dayton of New Jersey stated that when "assertion is given for proof and terror substituted for argument, they should have no effect however eloquently spoken." He further characterized the Virginia Plan as "a novelty," "an amphibious monster," and totally unacceptable to the people.[45] Gunning Bedford of the small state of Delaware, no longer able to contain himself, accused the large states of aggrandizement and made sarcastic remarks about the "diminutive State of Georgia" which was keeping an eye on possible future wealth and greatness; about South Carolina, puffed up by her wealth and negroes; and about North Carolina and Virginia.[46] He then blasted forth: "Pretences to support ambition are never wanting," and, "I do not trust you, gentlemen. The small States never can agree to the Virginia Plan. Why prolong the agony? Sooner than be ruined, there are foreign powers who will take us by the hand." Gouverneur Morris of Pennsylvania countered that the country must be united and, if persuasion could not do it, the sword would.[47] Apologies were suggested as appropriate for such heated outbursts. These are just a few samples of the bitterness that was engendered.

On July 2, a vote was taken on a resolution that in the second branch (Senate), each state should have an equal vote. Again North Carolina was with the big states in opposition. This was a tie vote, five to five, with Georgia divided.[48] William Pierce of Georgia had gone to New York to attend Congress, and to fight a duel with Alexander Hamilton as second to his adversary. Daniel Jenifer of Maryland was late in getting to the Convention. Both of these delegates had sided with the large states. Pierce's presence would have carried Georgia with the large States and Jenifer's presence would have divided Maryland, which voted with the small states. This absence and the sudden decision by Abraham Baldwin of Georgia to change his vote were a godsend.[49] With the ship of State almost on the rocks, General Charles Cotesworth Pinckney of South Carolina proposed that a committee consisting of one member from each State be appointed to consider and devise some form of Compromise.[50] The suggestion met hearty support. Dr. Hugh Williamson of North Carolina stated, "if we do not concede on both sides, our business must soon be at an end."[51] He favored the suggested reference to a committee, as he believed a small body would consider the question with more coolness and he was in favor of compromise. Luther Martin had no objection to a committee but said no change whatsoever could reconcile the smaller states to the least modification of their equal sovereignty. Sherman said that "we were now at a full stop;" but he added that nobody was for breaking up without accomplishing something.[52] The nationalist leaders, James Madison, James Wilson, and Governeur Morris, held out to the last against change in the Virginia Plan.[53] The tie vote was providential, because it left an opening for a compromise. The suggestion for reference to a committee, meeting with favor, accelerated chances for a compromise.

On the Grand Committee, as this special committee has since

been called, a representative from each state was elected by
Convention ballot. Colonel William R. Davie was selected the
representative for North Carolina, Elbridge Gerry for Massachu-
setts, Judge Oliver Ellsworth for Connecticut, Robert Yates for
New York, William Paterson for New Jersey, Dr. Benjamin
Franklin for Pennsylvania, Gunning Bedford for Delaware, Lu-
ther Martin for Maryland, George Mason for Virginia, John
Rutledge for South Carolina, and Abraham Baldwin for Georgia.[54]
Elbridge Gerry was made Chairman.[55] It was the second day of
July and adjourment was taken over July 4 and until Thursday, the
fifth, to allow cooling time. Richard Dobbs Spaight wrote to Judge
James Iredell that the Convention, thus far, had made but little
progress and that it was a matter of uncertainty when the business
would be finished.[56] One July 5 Elbridge Gerry, for the Committee, delivered its report. It was founded on a motion in the Grand
Committee by Dr. Franklin providing, among other things, in
substance: I. that there should be one representative for every
40,000 inhabitants, counting every five slaves as three free
inhabitants; II. that money bills and appropriations should originate in the House of Representatives, without alteration by the
second branch; and III. that, in the second branch, each state
should have an equal vote.[57] On these three propositions, North
Carolina did her best work.

Because the report consisted of propositions mutually condi-
tional and non-binding,[58] Nathaniel Gorham of Massachusetts
called for some explanation touching the ground on which the
conditions were based. Chairman Gerry stated that the Committee members were of different opinions and that they agreed to the
report merely in order that some kind of operating plan might be
proposed. He added that those opposed to an equal number of
votes in the Senate had only assented conditionally and if their
opponents did not generally agree, they would be under no
obligation to support the report.[59] Mr. Wilson thought that the
members of the Committee had exceeded their powers and

favored individual study of the questions presented. Otherwise, he declared, it would be a leap in the dark. Luther Martin of Maryland, one of the small state leaders, favored taking a vote at once on the whole report.[60] James Madison made a lengthy adverse discussion on the report, saying that with injustice and the minority on their side, the large states had everything to fear, as it was vain to propose concord in the Convention on terms which would perpetuate discord among their constituents. He said he could never become reconciled to equality in the Senate.[61] And Pierce Butler stated he opposed adopting a plan evidently unjust, and that he did not consider the concession concerning money bills as of any consequence.

It was at this point that Gouverneur Morris in a lengthy speech, said that this country must be united, either by peaceful agreement or by internal war. He further said that the scenes of horrow attending civil commotion cannot be described and that the conclusion of such a war "will be worse than the term of its continuance, as the stronger party will make traitors of the weaker and the gallows and halter will finish the work of the sword."[62] Junning Bedford of Delaware a leader of the small states, explained that his remarks at a prior time about some foreign power taking the small states by the hand had been misunderstood and that he did not mean the small states would court the aid and interposition of foreign powers; but that they would not consider the federal compact as dissolved until it should be done by the acts of the large states.[63] Dr. Williamson tried to smooth over some of the brash statements.[64] William Paterson acknowledged that the warmth of the members was improper, giving little credence himself to the sword and the gallows as being able to produce conviction. George Mason said that the report was meant not as specific propositions to be adopted; but merely as general grounds of consideration, as there must be some accommodation, or else little progress could be made in the work.[65] As North Carolina now began to take an important role in the proceedings, the propositions of the Grand Committee will be taken up in the order of their convention discussion.

The first proposition of the Grand Committee was that each of the States in the union should be allowed one member for every 40,000 inhabitants of the description reported in the 7th resolution of the Committee of the Whole House.[66] This resolution, reported to the House on June 13, was to the effect that the rights of suffrage in the first branch of the national legislature ought not to be according to the rule established in the Articles of Confederation but according to some equitable ratio of representation in proportion to the whole number of white and other free citizens, etc., and 3/5 of all other persons.[67]

Fixing a rule of representation in the first branch produced one of the real battles of the Convention, as it aroused questions as to whether or not apportionment of representatives should be based on numbers, or wealth, or both; whether or not slaves should be counted in computing population, and whether or not representation should be in accordance with taxation. On Friday, the 6th of July, Gouverneur Morris moved to commit that portion of the report relating to one member for every 40,000 inhabitants. He thought that the number of each state in the first instance might be absolutely fixed, leaving the legislature at liberty to provide for changes.[68] The question arose as to what would happen when other states should come into the Union, or when states already in the Union should be consolidated. Colonel Davie was for creating a Special Committee to get at the merits of the questions arising in connection with the report and he seemed to think that wealth, or property, ought to be represented in the second branch, or the Senate, and numbers in the first branch, or House.[69] By a vote of 7 to 3, Gouverneur Morris, Nathaniel Gorham, Edmund Randolph, John Rutledge and Rufus King were appointed on this Special Committee.[70]

The question of equality of votes in the Senate, or the third proposition of the Grand Committee was then taken up and Dr.

Franklin observed that this question could not be properly studied by itself as the Committee had reported several propositions as mutual conditions of each other, which precluded him from voting on the item separately, although he could vote for the whole report taken together.[71] It was then carried that action be postponed, until the Special Committee on representation, just above referred to, should report. Then the clause relating to originating money bills, the second proposition of the Grand Committee, was taken up.[72] In the Report it was not separately numbered.

This clause provided that all bills for raising or appropriating money and for fixing the salaries of the officers of the government of the United States should originate in the first branch of the legislature and should not be altered or amended by the second branch and that no money should be drawn from the public treasury unless in pursuance of appropriations originating in the first branch.[73] There was considerable discussion. Dr. Williamson, when this question was before the committee at a previous time, had spoken in favor of the proposition, saying that "it would oblige some member in the lower branch to move and the people could then mark him."[74] He now seemed to think that, if the appropriations privilege were not common to both branches, it ought rather be confirmed to the second (Senate) as bills in that case would be more narrowly watched.[75] Later he charged some of the small states with foresaking the condition on which they had received their equality in the Senate, stating that North Carolina had agreed to this equality merely in consideration that money bills should be confined to the other House.[76] It is said that Dr. Franklin devised this diplomatic scheme in the report of the Grand Committee in order to reach an agreement between the large and small states on equal representation in the Senate.[77] Reading between the lines, his diplomacy seems to have won over his fellow philosopher, Dr. Williamson. The provision was in accord with similar provisions of some state constitutions, taken from the British system. It was thought that the lower branch was closer to the people, who should hold the purse strings. James Madison, Rufus King of Massachusetts, Pierce Butler of South Carolina and others vigorously opposed stripping the Senate of such power.[78] A good deal was said about this being no concession at all, or at least an insufficient one, on the part of the small states. Others thought that such matters should be handled by both branches. It was the first proposal of the Grand Committee to be adopted, on July 6. This was effected by North Carolina voting with the smaller states of Connecticut, New Jersey, Delaware and Maryland.[79] North Carolina definitely was beginning to see the justice in the contentions of the small states and was likewise beginning to break the grasp of the large states upon her and to do a little independent thinking; but the question was to come up again, when a vote was to be taken on the full report.

On the 7th of July the delegates voted on whether equal Senate representation should stand as part of the report. Gerry of Massachusetts sensed the feeling of the Convention when he called this "the critical question."[80] He said that he would rather agree to it than have no accommodation. James Madison, Judge James Wilson, and Gouverneur Morris manfully contended for proportional representation. Judge Paterson doubted the value of the privilege concerning money bills, stating that unless there should be equality of votes in the second branch the small states would never be able to defend themselves so that there was no other acceptable ground for agreement. He said that his resolution was fixed and that he could meet the large states on the ground and none other. He further said that he would vote against the report because it yielded too much. The question as to whether equal representation in the Senate should stand as part of the report was carried by an affirmative vote of 6 to 3. North Carolina again voted with the small states. Several affirmative votes, however, were given because another final vote was to be taken on the whole report, to meet the mutuality of conditions on which the whole report was submitted.[81]

On the 9th of the July, Gouverneur Morris from the Committee of Five, to whom was referred the question of one representative for every 40,000 inhabitants, recommended that the first branch consist of 56 members, giving the number of representatives for each State.[82] This Committee also recommended that, as the situations of the states might be altered both in point of wealth and in numbers, the legislature be authorized from time to time to augment the number of representatives, depending upon changes in their wealth and population.[83]

Roger Sherman at once wanted to know "upon what principles or calculations" the report was founded as it did not appear to correspond with any rule of number or any representation hitherto adopted by Congress.[84] Mr. Gorham explained that the number of blacks and whites with some regard to supposed wealth made up the general rule. The Convention was now getting into deep water. Luther Martin wanted to know whether the committee were guided in the ratio by wealth or by number of inhabitants or by both; whereupon Morris and Rutledge moved to postpone the paragraph relating to the number of members to be allowed each state and to take up the second paragraph authorizing the legislature to alter the number from time to time according to wealth and inhabitants. This second paragraph on legislative alteration in the numbers allotted to each state was carried by a vote of 9 to 2.[85]

Mr. Sherman then moved to refer the first part of the report, apportioning the representatives, to another Grand Committee consisting of one member from each state. Dr. Williamson here remarked that it would be necessary to return to the rule of numbers; but it took the Convention a long time to digest the simplicity of this rule, though Judge Paterson considered the proposed estimate for the future according to the combined rule of numbers and wealth as too vague and stated that, for this reason, New Jersey was against it.[86] Another Grand Committee was then appointed, consisting of Rufus King, of Massachusetts, Roger Sherman of Connecticut, Robert Yates of New York, David

Brearley of New Jersey, Gouverneur Morris of Pennsylvania, George Reid of Delaware, Daniel Carroll of Maryland, James Madison of Virginia, Dr. Hugh Williamson of North Carolina, John Rutledge of South Carolina, and William Houston of Georgia.[87]

Mr. King, for this second Grand Committee, reported on July 10th that, in the original formation of the legislature of the United States, the first branch (House of Representatives) was to consist of 65 members, of which number New Hampshire would send 3, Massachusetts 8, Rhode Island 1, Connecticut 5, New York 6, New Jersey 4, Pennsylvania 8, Delaware 1, Maryland 6, Virginia 10, North Carolina 5, South Carolina 5, and Georgia 3.[88] North Carolina was given an equal state part, or 1/13th of the total of 65 fixed for the membership. Many motions were made and seconded to alter the numbers. Governor Martin of North Carolina moved that her quota be changed from 5 to 6. All of these motions were voted down. As the report raised the unsettled question "upon what principles or calculations" it was based, one of the most complicated debates of the whole Convention immediately followed. Some of these questions were: (1) should the ratio of representation be based on numbers, or wealth, or both; (2) should slaves be counted in estimating numbers, or wealth; and (3) should direct taxation be in accordance with representation. It is almost impossible to segregate these questions in the journal of the Convention and in the notes that were kept; but an effort will be made to do so.

It is doubtful if the Convention had in it a single member who favored anything like manhood suffrage, as we now know it. In the 1776 Constitution of North Carolina there were property qualifications for membership in the Senate of the General Assembly and for those qualified to vote for such officials. Many of the Convention delegates thought that property should play a leading part in fixing the ratio of representation. Gouverneur Morris stated that life and liberty were generally said to be of more value than property; but that an accurate view of the matter would prove that property was the main object of society, which Rutledge characterized as expressing some of his sentiments precisely, that property was certainly the principal object of society.[89] Rufus King and Purce Butler expressed like sentiments. Nathaniel Gorham and Charles Pinckney thought that numbers would be the best index. They knew that the rule in the Articles of Confederation using land and improvements thereon had been a failure as a basis for apportioning governmental expenses among the states. No method could be devised, they believed, to prevent the states from taking advantage of one another. Eliphalet Dyer of Connecticut vividly expressed the general feeling when he facetiously proposed in the Continental Congress that each of the States cheat equally.[90] After long debate Judge Wilson, the old Caledonian, queried (according to Madison's notes): "if numbers be not a proper rule why is not some better rule pointed out? No one has yet ventured to attempt it. Congress has never been able to discover a better." In 1783, after elaborate discussion of a measure of wealth, all were satisfied then as they are now that the rule of numbers does not differ much from the combined rule of numbers and wealth. Again, Judge Wilson could not agree that property was the sole or the primary object of government and society. He believed, "the cultivation and improvement of the human mind is the most notable object."[91] Wealth as a ratio of representation was finally eliminated by a large vote on July 13th.[92] But before then other elements like counting the slaves had been stumbling blocks in the paths of peace.

Mr. King had remarked on July 9 that, "as the Southern States are the richest, they would not league themselves with the Northern, unless some respect was paid to their superior wealth."[93] Randolph moved on the tenth "that, in order to ascertain the alterations in the population and wealth of the several states, the legislature should be required to cause a census etc. and arrange Representation accordingly.[94] Some called such a course shackling the legislature. Dr. Williamson then spoke up for making it the duty of the Legislature to do what was right and not leaving it at liberty to do or not do it. He moved postponement of Randolph's proposition in order to consider the following: "That, in order to ascertain the alterations that may happen in the population and wealth of the several States, a census shall be taken of the free white inhabitants and 3/5s of those of other descriptions on the first year after the Government shall have been adopted and every year thereafter; and, that the Representation be regulated accordingly."[95] This included "the 3/5th rule" for counting the slaves, heretofore mentioned as having been adopted by the Continental Congress (1783), in apportioning expenses between the states .[96] Randolph readily agreed that Dr. Williamson's proposition should be substituted for his.[97]

The debate on slaves was thus brought squarely before the Convention. Butler and General Pinckney were for including them equally in the population count. Gerry thought that 3/5 was at least sufficient allowance and Gorham referred to the historical fact that this ratio was fixed by Congress as a rule of taxation (1783).[98] Dr. Williamson reminded Gorham that, while the Southern states contended for the inferiority of the slaves, when taxation was involved the North fought for thier equality and further said that he did not then (1783) or now concur in either extreme, but approved the ratio of 3/5.[99] Dr. Williamson was a member of the Continental Congress when the rule was fixed to supplant "land and improvements" as a basis for apportionment of governmental expenses.[100] Bancroft says in his *History of the Constitution* that "The final concession on the representation for slaves proceeded from North Carolina." Williamson accepted for the permanent basis "the free inhabitants and 3/5 of all others".[101] This is the ratio that was finally adopted.

Gouverneur Morris stated in detail objections to Dr. Williamson's proposition; it would fetter the legislature and exclude some states altogether who had not enough population for one representative. He wished to override the plan already adopted, which left it to the Legislature to adjust from time to time the representation based on population and wealth. Later on, he said being reduced to the dilemma of doing injustice to the Southern states, or to human nature, he would do it to the former.[102] James Wilson could not well see on what principle the admission of the slaves in the proportion of 3/5th could be explained. If as citizens, then they should be on equality with other citizens. If as property, then why was other property not admitted? He agreed that these difficulties could be overcome by compromise.[103] Dr. Williamson's proposal for a census carried; but the 3/5 part of it was left open, until his whole proposal, as it would seem from Madison's notes, was voted down.[104] Then Colonel Davie said, (according to Madison's notes): "It is high time now to speak out." He saw that some delegates intended to deprive the Southern states of any share of representation for their blacks. He was sure that North Carolina would never confederate on any terms that did not rate slaves at least as 3/5s. If the Eastern states meant therefore to exclude them altogether he said, "the business is at an end."[105] The fight went on over wealth and numbers; over counting or not counting the blacks; over leaving it to the legislature to adjust, on basis of wealth and numbers, as agreed; over the entrance of new states; over the relation between taxation and representation; and so on. It is impossible to quote from all of the fine arguments that were presented, or from those that were not so fine, in the short space of this discussion. Colonel Davie's argument was most effective: Count the slaves as 3/5th, or "business was at an end."

Dr. Williamson had gotten on the right track when he expressed the simple, sensible thought that it would be necessary to return to the rule of numbers and he also helped considerably when he suggested a census, with the 3/5th rule for counting the blacks. Diplomacy caused negros to be referred to as "3/5 of those of other descriptions," or "3/5 of all other persons." But these Williamson proposals did not bring concord by themselves.

Counting the blacks as population in a formula for apportionment was obnoxious to some; making apportionment of sums for general welfare and defense, according to surveyed lands and improvements thereon, as in the Confederation, had been a failure. Now the principle of apportioning both taxation and representation on the basis of free population, including three-fifths of all other persons, or slaves, was taking a strong hold.

The old idea that representation and taxation should go hand in hand finally settled the debate. Gouverneur Morris moved to add to the clause already passed, empowering the Legislature from time to time to adjust representation according to numbers and wealth, a proviso that taxation should be in proportion to representation.[106] He changed this to "direct taxation."[107] It was contended that the rule of wealth should be ascertained and not left to the Legislature. Other unsatisfactory motions were made, until Randolph renewed the motion of Dr. Williamson calling for a census and rating the blacks at 3/5th.[108] Wilson observed that "less umbrage would perhaps be taken against the admission of slaves in the rule of representation, if it should be expressed as to make them indirectly only an ingredient in the rule, by saying that they should enter into the rule of taxation; and as representation was to be according to taxation, the end would be equally obtained."[109] Something more was said about making the blacks equal and other objections were raised; but Judge Wilson had about "knocked the fog off the situation." Wealth was stricken out and 3/5th of the slaves substituted as taxable and represented population. The motion for apportioning both representation and direct taxation on population, according to this interpretation, passed the Convention on July 13 by a vote of 9 to 0, and ended this controversy.[110] The provision as expressed in the final draft of the Constitution was as follows: "Representation and direct taxes shall be apportioned among the several states, ... according to their respective Numbers, which shall be determined by adding to the whole number of free Persons, ..., 3/5 of all other Persons."[111]

The same rule of apportionment for direct taxation and for representation seemed to produce the requisite impartiality that the states sought. Enlarging the population by unfair count would boost direct taxes and decreasing the population by similar methods would reduce representation. The North Carolina signers, in a letter to the Governor, expressed much satisfaction with this arrangement.[112] It seemed to be productive of fairness; but, as an actual fact, direct taxation amounted to very little. For forty years the Congress only levied three direct taxes[113] and, when the income tax laws were added, only four,[114] Direct taxation was considered the last resort. The Convention never dreamed of the modern philosophy of "getting money where the money is" and the most of it where extraction is easiest.

There were now only ten states represented in the Convention. After the tenth of July, the vote of New York was no longer entered on the Journal. Lansing and Judge Yates tired of listening to the delegates from the big states like Madison, Morris, King, Wilson and others and, feeling that the Convention was exceeding its authority, left it never to return.[115] Alexander Hamilton temporarily left the floor. He was not in accord with this colleagues, who represented the sentiment of the ruling party in New York. This threw out the vote of New York. The New Hampshire delegation had not yet arrived and Rhode Island was never represented in the Convention.

On July 14, Luther Martin called for a decision on the whole report of the Grand Committee. All that day and the following the contending forces were in a death grapple over the "Connecticut Compromise" for equality in the Senate. On the 16th the Convention voted on the whole Report and the Report of the Grand Committee, as amended, passed by a five to four decision, with Massachusetts divided and with Connecticut, New Jersey, Delaware, Maryland, and North Carolina in the affirmative, and Pennsylvania, Virginia, South Carolina, and Georgia in the negative. This ended the Great Crisis. The deciding vote was cast by the State of North Carolina. It was the most important vote cast in the Convention.[116] Indeed it was one of the most important decisive votes ever cast in a law-framing body, because it saved the Convention and the Constitution. North Carolina was the real balance wheel among her sister states in the Federal Convention that formed our Constitution.

Honorable Hannis Taylor, in his excellent work on *The Origin and Growth of the American Constitution*, says that victory was won "by the bold and determined stand taken by North Carolina in favor of justice to the smaller States."[117] Mr. Bancroft says that the decision was made by North Carolina which broke the grip of the large States and gave a majority of one to the smaller states.[118] Burton J. Hendrick in his *Bulwarks of the Republic*, (1937), is incisive: "Those looking for the hidden motive behind this accommodation should observe one enlightening fact—that North Carolina though the third largest State and sympathetic with Virginia throughout the Convention, cast its vote for the 'Connecticut Compromise.' Up to the final moment this delegation had stood firm against the proposal; its sudden switch, however, made the Connecticut idea victorious by a vote of 5 to 4—one of those 5 to 4 decisions which, when exercised by the Supreme Court in recent years, have stirred revolutionary emotions."[119] John Fiske, in *The Critical Period of American History*, for some unaccountable reason, gives the credit to Massachusetts, because Elbridge Gerry and Caleb Strong on one side and Rufus King and Nathaniel Gorham on the other split that state's vote and caused it to be thrown out.[120] In this great speech on the "Constitution and Its Makers" before the Literary and Historical Association of North Carolina, in Raleigh on November 28, 1911, Senator Henry Cabot Lodge refers to the part taken by "Your State and Mine;" but he mentions no detail about North Carolina. How appropriate it would have been at least to have mentioned her deciding vote in the great crisis. It was the change that North Carolina made in her voting and not the failure of Massachusetts to vote that carried the question for the small States. Massachusetts was negative; North Carolina was positive and effective.

Charles Warren, of Massachusetts another of our most distinguished writers on the Constitution, while he placed very little stress on North Carolina's vote, says that, had the Connecticut Compromise failed, the Convention would have failed; for it was certain that the delegates from the small states would have left the Convention had the vote been otherwise.[121] Colonel Davie, a leader in the Hillsboro, North Carolina, convention, when asked to comment upon the Federal Constitution, which he had helped to frame, gave as his opinion "that the protection of the small states against the ambition and influence of the larger members could have been effected only by arming them with the equal power in one branch of the legislature." "On a contemplation of this matter," said he, "we shall find that the jealousies of the States could not have been reconciled in any other way. The lesser States would never had concurred, unless this check against the power and encrochment of the great States had been given to the small States, as a security for their political existence."[122]

It will be seen that some of the greatest writers on the framing of the Federal Constitution have credited North Carolina with this decisive vote. It is North Carolina delegates, who left the large states with whom they naturally belonged, and went with the small states in justice to their rights which they determined by the North Carolina vote.

It is difficult to state, categorically, just who influenced the North Carolina delegation to change its allegiance from the large states to the small states. Colonel Davie and Dr. Williamson were the only members of the North Carolina delegation who had anything of record to say on the subject, either in or out of the Convention. William Blount was in New York attending the Continental Congress from July 4 to August 3, where he had been summoned to make a quorum. He left the Convention on the

advice and with the consent of the other delegates.[130] Soon after
he left, on July 19, three days after the final vote, he wrote to his
brother, John Gray Blount, that he had left Dr. Hugh Williamson
at he head of the delegation.[131] The record shows that Mr. Spaight
was against the compromise.[132] It is not definitely known how
Governor Alexander Martin stood. There is no record; but he
must have voted for the compromise, because, had he done
otherwise, the North Carolina delegation would have stood two to
two, on the Report of the Grand Committee, and the State thus
would have lost its vote, as did Massachusetts. Col. Davie and
Gov. Martin, though they left the Convention in August, were
strong adovcates of adoption when both of the North Carolina
Conventions were called to ratify or reject the Constitution. Gov.
Martin was defeated for membership in the Hillsboro Convention
on account of his views on the Constitution and was just about to
enter a term as Governor of North Carolina during the Fayetteville Convention. He was strongly in favor of ratification. There is
no doubt but that Col. Davie played a large part in effecting this
controlling vote and it may have been the leading part, due to the
fact that he was North Carolina's representative on the Grand
Committee; but there is nothing in the record to indicate he may
be given the entire credit. However, he did give such a signal in
his speech in the Federal Convention, when he said that if he were
required to vote on the comparative merits of the report, as it
stood, and the and the amendment (equal senate vote), he would
feel constrained to vote for the Connecticut idea. Sometime after
the vote on the floor of the Convention, Dr. Williamson gave as a
reason for North Carolina's change, Dr. Franklin's suggestion
about the House originating money bills.[133] Dr. Williamson was
on another Grand Committee to reconsider Representation in the
House, as provided in the report of the first Grand Committee,
before the whole report was finally voted upon. He expressed
dissatisfaction with the report when it first came in on July 5, but
advocated discussion and compromise. Colonel Davie first ex-

pressed some dissatisfaction with the Connecticut Compromise; but, like Dr. Williamson, he was in favor of some kind of compromise. they both must have felt the justice and the necessity of the Connecticut idea, in order to get some form of a Constitution which they were there to frame.

North Carolina through her delegates, acted with great wisdom and forethought, though she has never received due credit for her contribution to the framing of our Constitution. A month after the Compromise settlement, Dr. Hugh Williamson, the "Honest Doctor", as he was styled by his friend Washington Irving,[134] wrote to Governor Caswell that, on some future occasion, the delegates would be at liberty to explain how difficult a role had fallen to North Carolina and that they had sustained it with a principle and firmness that should entitle them to the thanks of the public, though such thanks would never be asked.[135] What a pity none of them ever told in detail the whole story of the part they played. What a pity it is that we do not have a better written picture of the secret meetings, manipulations, trades, and outside adjustments that went into the making of the Constitution.

Most of the arrangement and language and many of the provisions of the Constitution were worked out by the Committee of Detail;[136] the Committee of Eleven, on postponed parts of the Constitution and parts of the Reports not acted upon;[137] the Committee of Revision;[138] and the Committee of Style.[139] Dr. Williamson was a member of the Committee of Eleven which made a full report and occupied the Convention from September 1 to September 5.[140]

The main point is that North Carolina, one of the large states, at the most critical period of the Convention, changed her position and cast for the small states the deciding vote which saved the Convention and the Constitution. Her controlling action, in a five to four decision, made the Connecticut Compromise a reality. Otherwise, it might have been only a dream.

One great statesman has said that the Constitution had its origin in the good sense of able men, applied to the practical work in hand,[141] and Mr. Robert Morris, one of the able framers, remarked: "I have many reasons to believe that it is the work of plain, honest men and such, I think it will appear."[142] North Carolina's delegates certainly used more good sense than has ever been credited to them.

There were countless conflicts to be adjusted in the many crises that arose during the Convention, which continued to sit for two more months, until September 17. It is the object of the writer to give some emphasis to the principal thing which North Carolina did in this Convention. Less important details will be taken up in the sketches of the delegates, most of whom made remarks as the Convention progressed; but the remarks were of little practical importance when compared with their work in the settlement of the Great Crisis. It has been thought best not to mention in this Chapter the disconnected remarks and thus water the cream to the point where the article would be almost unpalatable.

It would be folly to minimize the differences that arose between the so-called agricultural and industrial sections, with both having visions of territorial expansion. It is difficult to arrange Convention disputes along geographical lines, especially when we recognize the little known fact that the Piedmont Section of the Carolinas, usually considered entirely agricultural, had been styled the cradle of manufacturing industry in this country and one of the first areas to combat slavery. For instance, the early settlers of Rowan County, on August 8, 1774, in their patriotic resolves passed by the first meeting of a Committee of Safety in North Carolina, took the lead in denouncing slavery as economically unsound and as an obstruction to the settlement of foreign manufacturers among them. They declared themselves favorable to manufacturing industries as a "badge of distinction, respect, and true patriotism."[143] Daniel Augustus Tompkins of Charlotte, said: "When I left South Carolina to go North, I thought I was leaving a country which had never had any important manufactures. Later, when I was in the middle of industrial life in the North, I conceived the idea of writing an industrial history of the United States. To my amazement I found that the agricultural South, from which I had come in a spirit of industrial despair, was the cradle of maufactures in the United States."[144]

There were serious clashes over lodgement of control of commerce between the states and with foreign countries. From these commercial wrangles between the several states sprang the Mount Vernon Compact and the Annapolis Trade Convention out of which grew the Philadelphia Convention. Before, during, and after the Revolution there were wide local divergences between the ever-present Whig and Tory factions. Then there were the battles over slavery, the slave traffic, and the fierce fight over the method of counting the slaves in arriving at apportionment of representatives in the more numerous body of the legislative branch. There was also the dispute over treaty-making power and the participation of the executive and legislative branches in it. Every detail of the Constitution was discussed at length, including the permanent location of the capital of the United States. North Carolina's delegates made remarks on most of these subjects.

In the Convention these antagonistic seekers after truth, contending for it as they conceived it to be, produced the blessed checks and balances which ever since have so strengthened the Union's fundamental law. It is certain, above all else, that they wanted to frame a government under which men could be free.

"They wished men to be free
As much from mobs as kings
From you as me".

Among all of these conflicting minds in the Constitutional Convention, striving for adjustments in the new alignment, the forecasted difficulty on representation in the legislative branch appears to have been the most troublesome. The delegates sought to distribute power in its endless details among independent legislative, executive, and judicial departments. How shall we vote?[145] That was the big question. North Carolina did her part, both as to the House of Representatives and as to the Senate. Her prominent role in the battle to restore the power to originate money bills to the House of Representatives—Dr. Benjamin Franklin's key which unlocked the mystery of representation— was another contribution to the Federal Convention of 1787.[146]

Chapter 2

SOME INFORMATION

About Governor William Blount,
Governor Alexander Martin,
Governor William Richardson Davie,
Governor Richard Dobbs Spaight, and
Dr. Hugh Williamson

*With Notations of Some of the Provisions of the
Constitution Suggested by North Carolina Delegates*

NOTE

Very little has been written about the individual contributions to the language of the Constitution by the North Carolina delegates. In fact, there are to be found very few articles in the Constitution, or even parts thereof, originating with them. However, there are a few. Some mention will be made of them. It is thought that a few details of the lives of our delegates may not be inappropriate. The delegates will be taken up in the order in which they usually are arranged.

The illustrations accompanying the sketches of Governor Blount, Governor Martin, and Governor Spaight were prepared from plates etched by Mr. Albert Rosenthal for the history of the 100th Anniversary of the promulgation of the Constitution of the United States, edited by Hamilton L. Carson, Secretary of the Constitutional Centennial Commission, Philadelphia, 1889. The others, Governor William Richardson Davie and Dr. Hugh Williamson, respectively, were prepared by Mr. Rosenthal for this work. Our thanks are proffered for their use herein.

WILLIAM BLOUNT
1744-1800

There are no Constitutional provisions that were suggested by William Blount. Much of his time during the Convention was spent in New York. He did, however, make a statement of importance in the closing days of the Convention.

When Mr. Blount was appointed a delegate, he was a member of the Continental Congress, sitting in New York, being then prominently mentioned for its President.[1] Frequently he was the sole representative in that body from North Carolina. However, he kept in touch with his colleagues in Philadelphia.[2] He was present in the Convention during the last month of its duration. He traveled to the Philadelphia Convention from New York on June 20 and returned to New York for the period from July 2 to August 6, on urgent congressional call and upon advice and consent of his fellow delegates.[3] At the solicitation of Secretary Thomson, he got back to New York in time to help enact the Northwest Ordinance, on July 13, 1787, one of the most important acts of the Continental Congress.[4] On August 20 he wrote Governor Caswell that, while he could not disclose what was going on, the form of Government "will be such as will be their (the States) respective interest to adopt." He added that he might have to go back to New York, if other representatives did not appear there. He hoped that Robert Burton would arrive there to join John B. Ashe. If they were not there, he concluded, he would consider it his duty to be in New York, disagreeable and inconvenient though it might be, to see that North Carolina was sufficiently represented, to receive and to recommend to the states the result of the Constitutional Convention's work. A staunch Federalist, he did return and joined with others in the Congress in recommending the work of the Convention to the states.[5] In the Congress he was succeeded by his colleague, Dr. James White, the grandfather of Chief Justice Edward Douglas White.

At the close of the Federal Convention, he helped to remove the last barrier to signing the Constitution and no doubt relieved the anxiety of many members by assuring the house that, while he had said that he would not sign the Constitution as this might bind his support as an individual, he was willing to attest the fact that the plan was the unanimous act of the states in Convention.[6] These remarks followed a statement from Alexander Hamilton, aroused by Dr. Williamson's suggestion that delegates sign a letter of transmittal to the Continental Congress. Hamilton remarked that a few characters of consequence, by refusing to sign, might do infinite mischief.[7] Such diplomatic procedure first suggested by Dr. Franklin on the last day of the Convention, to get timid and faltering members to sign favorably may be properly appraised when it is remembered that sixteen of the fifty-five attending members never signed the Constitution and that Elbridge Gerry, George Mason, and Governor Edmund Randolph, outstanding leaders, present at the end, absolutely refused to sign. Mr. Blount was for law and order and fully realized from personal experience the deficiencies of the old Articles of Confederation. As was customary, with his nature, he was for conciliation at a time when conciliation was of prime importance.

William Blount was not such a student of the many theories and philosophies of government as were others in the Convention; but he was thoroughly experienced in the field of practical politics both in his own state and in national affairs. He must have realized that the proposed Constitution, defective though it then seemed, was the best way out. He remained in his seat, and, as above said, signed it together with Spaight and Dr. Williamson. His colleague, Pierce of Georgia, who made pen pictures of the delegates, said that Blount was a character strongly marked for integrity and character, but that he had no talent as a speaker. He was then about thirty-six years old.[8]

William Blount was not a member of the Hillsboro, North Carolina Convention (1788) which refused unconditional ratification of the Constitution, because as a pro-constitution candidate he was defeated; but his brother, John Gray Blount and his cousins, Edmund Blount of Chowan, Edmund Blount of Tyrell,

Seth and Thomas Harvey, and Thomas Reading were there, all staunchly supporting adoption of the Constitution. His uncle William Gray of Bertie was also a member, and no doubt favored the Constitution, though his vote is not recorded. Blount was a member of the North Carolina ratifying convention at Fayetteville, (1789), representing Pitt County and some Tennessee Counties, with his brothers, John Gray Blount and Thomas Blount and a number of close kinsmen.[9] Here he seconded the motion of Dr. Williamson to read the Constitution.

The family to which William Blount belonged had been distinguished in England since the days of the Norman Conquest. At the time of the Convention, it had been located in North Carolina longer than any other family whose surname was then extant. So stated Henry Toole Clark, Governor of North Carolina during the War Between the States. "This ancient family," says Blount's biographer, General Marcus J. Wright, "has given birth to three distinct races of Peers," which he names. It has been said that the Blounts were of the same general Cavalier stock as the Washington family. Indeed, one of General George Washington's seventeenth century grandmothers was Constance Blount, a daughter of Sir Walter Blount, who was created a baronet by Charles I and suffered much in the cause of the House of Stuart. The two branches of the North Carolina family can claim the same descent, through two of her brothers, if the printed records are to be believed. Love of land was just as much a part of the English nature as the air which they breathed and into this atmosphere William Blount was born in his mother's old home in Bertie County, North Carolina, on March 26, 1749. His mother was Barbara Gray, whose father, John Gray, "a Scottish gentleman," came to North Carolina about 1700.[10] William was not a college man; but he received at home and in nearby academies at New Bern early educational advantages in keeping with the times and the high social and financial standing of his family. However he could lay no claims to being a learned scholar. Meeting the leading men of the Colony, engaging in plantation talk, and hearing about the vast land speculations to the westward were the methods by which he gained his education. When the town of Boonesboro, Kentucky, was established, his younger brother John Gray Blount, then scarcely of age, was in the Kentucky Country, in company with Daniel Boone, to find out what it was all about.[11] The trend of William Blount's mind was towards business rather than literary pursuits. Like George Washington, John Marshall and others of similar conservative mental bent, he must have admired such poetry as "Order is Heaven's First Law," and "The Proper Study of Mankind is Man." He graduated with honor in the school which studies and fathoms the minds and thoughts of contemporary actors and he became accomplished in the art of leading men.

He was born into a period which was heavily fraught with mischief both in politics and in war and he plunged with his vigorous manhood into these fields when quite young. In the company of the Royal Governor, his father Colonel Jacob Blount, and his brother, John Gray, he was at the Battle of Alamance in 1771 to silence the disturbances caused by the unfortunate Regulators in the central part of the colony. In Colonel Blount's accounts on this expedition, it appears that the militia mobilized under the command of Governor Tryon without regalia of any kind and in their every-day clothes which were "washed at Mr. Holt's".[12] Both he and his father were paymasters in the Continental Line and William was entrusted with similar duties throughout the Revolution. Though William never joined, both his father and his brother, Major Reading Blount, were original members of the North Carolina Society of the Cincinnati, of which General Washington was President-General during his life.[13]

William Blount was a member of the firm of John Gray Blount and Thomas Blount, merchants. The partnership which he had with these two brothers did business along the Atlantic Seaboard and England, Ireland, Spain, France, Holland, and the West Indies. Letters from Major James Cole Mountflorence, a Frenchman who was major of North Carolina troops in General Jethro Sumner's brigade, were published in the July 1937 issue of the *North Carolina Historical Review*. Major Mountflorence seems to have been a representative of the firm. He wrote from London, Paris, and Switzerland and a review of his letters will give some idea of the extent of the firm's operations, the names of their boats, and the nature of their business. This may seem unbelievable at this day, but at that time the shallow craft plying the ocean lanes could get in and out of Ocracoke and other North Carolina inlets. Blount, Spaight, and Williamson boasted in a letter to Governor Caswell, while in the Federal Convention, that North Carolina could build her own boats and take care of her own shipping, without leaning on others.[14] Governor William Blount's brothers, John Gray Blount, Colonel Thomas Blount, Major Reading Blount, and Governor Willie (pronounced Wiley) Blount were distinguished contemporaries.

Ownership of the land and speculation in it, together with politics, were the most engaging pursuits for a young gentleman situated as was William Blount. Early in his career he espoused the cause of the over-the-mountain boys and continued to do so throughout his life. Land companies and associations had been the order of the day since the early colonies had sprung from them. Such organizations were still operating in the colonies and in the early states along the seaboard. They were numerous. The Ohio Company was a large political and land speculating group started in 1786. It was made up mostly of New England Revolutionary leaders with Manasseh Cutler, a friend of Dr. Williamson and of the same comprehensive attainments, doing most of the promoting and lobbying to gain control of one and a half million acres on the Ohio and its tributaries. The Transylvania Company, similar to the other, was headed by Judge Richard Henderson and made up of such prominent North Carolinians as Nathaniel,

Thomas, and David Hart, Jesse Benton, John Williams, Leonard Henly Bullock, James Hogg, John Luttrell, William Johnston, Samuel and Nathaniel Henderson, Valentine Searcy, and others, all of whom were either associates or in some way connected with the company. They had the services of the best known of our early explorers, Daniel Boone, who resided in the Yadkin Valley in Rowan County, not far distant from Christopher Gist. There were many other well known associations like the Loyal Land Company of Virginia, with Dr. Thomas Walker at its head, and others too numerous to mention. Most of the well-to-do citizens on the Atlantic seaboard were agog about western lands.

The original fur-trading, colonizing, and land speculating group known as the Ohio Company, and headed largely by the Washingtons, should not be overlooked. This company was one of the first and was formed in 1749. Down in the Yadkin Valley, at Mulberry Fields, Rowan County, North Carolina, near where the town of Wilkesboro is now situated, lived Captain Christopher Gist, one of the greatest Indian scouts and guides of his day. He was the Ohio Company's agent to explore and map out its holding of some 500,000 acres.[15] Blount also had large interests with his collaborators in the Muscle Shoals section.[16]

The Blounts, however, seem principally to have been individual operators. John Gray was the landed nabob of these brothers.[17] They entered western lands in Kentucky and to the southward at an early period. William Blount was in touch with most of these western operators, was on familiar terms with many of them, and kept abreast with everything that was taking place. He selected as his agent Mr. James Robertson from Wake County, one of the first pioneers in the Holston and Wautauga settlements. For ten years James Robertson was the leader of these pioneers. He then moved on to the Cumberland Valley and deserves to be remembered as the Nestor of the Tennessee Wilderness. Blount made one contract with Robertson to purchase and make entry for 50,000 acres which the latter was to survey and locate, receiving therefore one-fourth of the lands. Robertson named one of his sons William Blount, another James White, and both of these sons became distinguished in Louisiana. The story goes that the two-horse fellows generally stopped in East Tennessee, while those with four horses moved on to the Cumberland.[18] The powerful Caswell political group to which Governor Blount belonged, headed by Richard Caswell and others, were particular about getting lands which they could hold and usually took their titles from the State of North Carolina, where they had sufficient political influence to back their claims. Titles in those days, with the conflicting interests of the old colonies and the states, the Indians, and the English, Spanish, and French Governments, were cloudy in the extreme and difficult to maintain.

During Blount's legislative career in North Carolina as representative from New Bern in 1780, from Craven County in 1783, and as a Senator from Pitt in 1788 and 1789, he was an active and efficient member of the General Assembly. When the Congress of the United States negotiated with the Indians the Hopewell Treaty in 1785, Colonel Blount, who was appointed the North Carolina representative to cooperate with the federal government, was present in person; but he vigorously protested the terms of the treaty and continued his opposition to the Congress, which ratified the pact. It delivered, he thought, too much land to the Indians, already entered or purchased by the whites.

A glance at the index to the State Records is sufficient to establish his importance in the General Assembly. He was always interested in education and was elected by the General Assembly a trustee of New Bern Academy, a trustee of the Academy of Kinston, and a trustee of Pitt Academy. He was also elected one of the original trustees of the University of North Carolina. Blount was also in favor of ceding the western lands of North Carolina to the national government, on proper terms. This was a live issue among the new states. In 1784 Thomas Jefferson wrote to James Madison: "We hope that North Carolina will cede. . . . For God's sake push this at the next session of the assembly." There was considerable discontent over the vast holdings of lands to the westward by some of the states. Blount was Speaker of the House of Commons in the spring Session of 1784 and worked zealously for the passage of the Cession Act of that year. After repeal of the first act, he played an important role in 1789 in the passage of the second act, ceding the western lands.[19]

While a member of the Continental Congresses of 1782, 1783, and 1786, 1787, he was one of the champions of the western interests and won for himself many friends among the early settlers across the mountains. He was elected as a member of Congress for 1784; but that year he was Speaker of the House in the General Assembly and doubtless declined. In 1787, when the Northwest Ordinance was passed, he voted against the admission of slavery into the area, as expressed in Article 6 of the Ordinance, prohibiting the institution. Although this section was later left out of the Act creating the Southwest Territory, nevertheless, in his addresses while organizing his territorial government, he read article 6 before his hearers without mentioning its omission in his territory.[20] Mention has been made of his part in the Continental Congress, in passing and acting upon the call for the Federal Convention. After the Federal Constitution became operative, his interests were transferred to the western country.

On June 8, 1790, President Washington appointed William Blount "Governor in and over the Territory of the United States South of the River Ohio," for the term of three years. He was again appointed on December 10, 1794, for another term of three years. He was also made Superintendent of Indian Affairs for the Southern District, the powers, duties, and emoluments of this office having been united with those of Governor under the Act for the Government of the territory. There were others who offered for the governorship, such as General Anthony Wayne and General Joseph Martin, the latter being urged by Governor Patrick Henry, Mr. Richard Henry Lee, William Grayson, Theodorick Bland, and others from Virginia.

Mr. Blount was very popular in the Territory and no doubt was more familiar with it than any of them. He was sponsored by the active and influential Territorial resident, General Daniel Smith, whom Washington subsequently made Secretary of the Territory. Smith was congratulated by Blount's diplomatic friend from France, Major James Cole Mountflorence, (said to have been an agent of Governor Davie,) then practising law at Nashville, where he was soon to end his eventful American career while busily wrestling, on the defense side of the docket, with the engaging details of a breach of promise suit. When they were interrogated by the President, Blount received the flattering endorsements of the North Carolina representatives in Congress, Timothy Bloodworth, John B. Ashe, and his friend and political colleague, Dr. Hugh Williamson. The latter referred to the fact that Blount had considerable lands in the Territory and that Blount must therefore be deeply interested in the area's success and prosperity. It is said that William Blount returned 73,252 acres for taxes when the State of Tennessee was formed and that he and Colonel Thomas Hart had some tens of thousands of acres in the Henderson, or Transylvania claims, in Kentucky. There is perhaps no accurate record; but it is very doubtful if William Blount took on any more lands after he was appointed Governor, as this gubernatorial task was enough to consume all of his energy, tact, and ability. He said in a letter to Governor Caswell on the 19th day of October 1786, that he had not purchased any lands from the Indians nor been so concerned, directly or indirectly, since June, 1785. Governor Blount wrote to General John Steele on July 10, 1790, thanking him for his congratulations and for his very active and friendly part in the appointment. He stated that the appointment was important to him as his Western lands had become so essential to him that it had become absolutely necessary to go the the western country to secure them. He also said that his presence might enhance their value. General Washington, too, was a holder of

considerable lands to the westward. Having property or being
financially responsible was, with General Washington, no deter-
rent to holding office. Governor Blount had served in the Constitutional Convention with General Washington, who had some
notions of his own as to Blount's "patriotism, integrity, and
abilities," to use the more or less stereotyped language of his
commission.[21]

The Territory South of the River Ohio comprised what is now
the States of Kentucky and Tennessee. It was then commonly
known as the Cherokee Country, though there were other tribes
claiming interest in it. When Blount entered upon his duties as
governor, a movement was already well under way for the
admission of Kentucky into the Union as a state. The new state
was admitted in 1792. Governor Blount's activities were confined
almost exclusively to the North Carolina land in the territory.

Governor Blount did not receive his commission until July 6,
1790 and could not get a copy of the ordinance for the government
of the Territory until August 18, as there was no copy in North
Carolina. He did not have a copy of the proclamation announcing
the acceptance by Congress of the second deed of Cession which
he considered necessary in view of the prior unpleasantness along
this line, so he proceeded to the home of Governor Alexander
Martin in Guilford. He sent Major George Farragut with a copy of
the ordinance and other papers to the Territory. The Major was
the father of Admiral Farragut and had been an outstanding North
Carolina soldier throughout the Revolutionary War. This was
about September 6. Mr. Blount wended his way to Philadelphia
for further instructions and information. He stopped at Mount
Vernon and paid President Washington a visit of several days. At
Alexandria on September 20, 1790, he took the oath of office
before Justice James Iredell, one of the most eminent of Carolinians and then a Justice of the Supreme Court of the United
States.[22]

In a lively letter written from Mount Vernon to his brother,

John Gray Blount, he gives an interesting account of the President, his family, and their delightful surroundings. Mrs. Washington was certainly one of the most agreeable women in the world. Major Washington, the general's nephew, was a handsome, genteel, attractive man and the Custis children were very promising. The house was not elegant, being first begun on too small a scale; but it was now very roomy and commodious and the dining room was very large and elegant. Mt. Vernon was highly improved, with a number of necessary outbuildings and good gardens. The Lombardy Poplar of which Ovid sang many years ago was very much admired; the tree helped to shade the delightful walks, straight, circular, and serpentine. He went on further: "Except the President is too awful (full of awe), I verily believe he is as awful as a God, Mount Vernon is the most agreeable place I ever saw." In this letter was also predicted the President's Southern Tour, in 1791, information regarding which he had elicited at the request of Governor Martin. He told his brother to prepare for "Pompous orders for equipping and training the Cavalry;" to "give Sam Simpson notice that he may have his Company in complete order;" and to have the overseers "mend their ways," and fix the roads and bridges, and build new boats. Some of these admonitions bore fruit as General Washington, with a touch of humor, or sarcasm, or both, remarked in his *Diary of His Southern Tour*, that, at Tarborough, he received "as good a salute as could be given by one piece of artillery," and that in Pitt County, where the Jacob Blount Mansion stood, "another small party of horse under one Simpson met us at Greenville, and in spite of every endeavor which could comport with decent civility to excuse myself from it, they would attend me to Newbern." The dust kicked up by General Simpson's troop of horse must have been unbearable; but even Washington's efforts could not check the enthusiasm the people felt for him. And Thomas Blount returned the compliment to his brother by entertaining the President at his handsome home in Tarboro.[23]

With these graceful preliminaries behind him, Governor William Blount took the meandering trail to the wilderness country. He reached the home of William Yancey in the territory on October 11, 1790, and immediately launched upon the multifarious duties which he had assumed among these steel-fibered pioneers in the Over-the-Hills Country.

Looking after the Indians did not take all of Governor Blount's time. He gave much attention to building up the territory. Under the Ordinance for the Government of the Southwest Territory the people were entitled to have representatives in a General Assembly as soon as the territory should have a population of 5,000 free male inhabitants. Governor Blount called for elections of representatives on October 19, 1793. He was instrumental in selecting the site and in founding and naming the town of Knoxville when he fixed the seat of his government at White's Fort in the wilderness. The *Knoxville Gazette*, said to have been the first newspaper in Tennessee, was promoted by him as an official organ of the Territory, and did valiant work in educating his constituents along the line of good government. In Knoxville in 1794, he was also one of the benefactors and founders of Blount College, the first coeducational institution and the first strictly non-denominational college in the country, so claimed, and now the University of Tennessee. It was chartered by the first assembly of the new territory on September 10, 1794. One of the principal buildings of the present University honors the name of his daughter, Barbara Blount, who it is said was the first woman student in the United States to be entered in such a higher seat of learning, though in its early existence Blount College was doubtless not much more than a good academy. Justice Sanford of the Supreme Court of the United States in his History of Blount College says that the whole college hill was subsequently called "Barbara Hill," in honor of Miss Blount. He further says that, while some of the girls attained one or two of the marks of distinction, the charming Barbara alone gained all of them and was recorded as not only "attentive" but also as "diligent" and "ingenious," for which "our historian accredited it no wonder that she captured the distinguished Major General Edmund Pendleton Gaines," of the United States Army and the hero of Fort Erie, for whom numerous towns in the South have been named.[24]

After organizing his territory and putting it into governmental form, one of his first important endeavors was to effect the Treaty of Holston. Following lengthy negotiations in July, 1791, Governor Blount assembled the Indians in great numbers at his home at the White Fort, now Knoxville, and brought about the Holston Treaty. Under this treaty the titles of the Creeks and Cherokees to most of the land in Tennessee were thought to have been extinguished. However, he was in constant trouble with the Indians for years yet to come. Suffice it to say that the hostile Creeks called him "Tucke Mico," the "Dirt King," and the more friendly Cherokees, "The Dirt Captain." There is now a bronze marker in the Court House square in Knoxville commemorating the successful outcome of this treaty. The ratifying Senate and the President of the United States, through the secretary of State, tendered to Governor Blount their thanks for his zeal in uniformly promoting the interests of the United States on the basis of justice and humanity to all parties concerned. His administration of the Southwest Territory has been published by the national government in book form.[25]

Many letters in Governor Blount's correspondence have been preserved. Among them is a breezy, convivial one, dated at Lexington, Kentucky, in 1795, from Colonel Thomas Hart, "not only a polished member of society but almost an accomplished and complete gentlemen," who had gone there from Hillsboro, North Carolina, as one of the original members of the Transylvania Company. Colonel Hart invited Governor Blount to move his family to "the finest country in the world" and went on to say: "Oh, if my old friend, Uncle Jacob, (father of William Blount) was but living in this country, what pleasure we should have in raking up the money and spending it with our friends!'' And further: ''There is not a day that passes over our heads but I can have half a dozen strange gentlemen to dine with us and they are from all parts of the Union.'' Colonel Hart's wife was the niece of Colonel Jacob Blount and Colonel Hart was the favorite uncle who furnished his own niece with the given name for her son, Senator Thomas Hart Benton. Colonel Hart's daughter, Lucretia, was the wife of Senator Henry Clay. Colonel Hart and Governor Blount held some of the Transylvania lands in common. Colonel Hart expressed the common urge when he humorously but truthfully said that, though 65 years old, he ''never would be satisfied in the world, while new countries could be found.''[26]

To reconcile the animosities of the Indians, the disagreements between the frontiersmen, the machinations of the Spanish authorities on his border, and the dilatory and clogging tactics of the general government at Washington, was an undertaking for any man. It required a high order of ability to perform his tasks. The Tennessee historian Ramsey, graphically summarizes the situation:[27]

> ''Some judgment may be formed of the difficult, responsible, and delicate duties which the two offices devolved on the Governor, by a brief reference to the posture of affairs when he received his appointments. . . .

> ''To reconcile all these animosities between savages, and to protect the Territory from their injurious effects, required frequent conferences and correspondence imposing a Herculean labor upon Mr. Blount. His correspondence with Governors of adjoining States, with the Secretary of War, and with the authorities of Spain, is extensive and minute. . . .

> ''To keep the Indian tribes quiet, to conciliate their friendship to the United States, to save the Territory

from invasion and to neutralize and prevent foreign influence, and at the same time not to jeopardize negotiations then pending, required a high degree of administrative capacity and diplomatic talent. In these arduous duties he was aided by his two private secretaries, Willie Blount and Hugh Lawson White.''

Governor Blount called a constitutional convention to meet in Knoxville on the 11th day of January, 1796. He was elected president of this convention, called to form the State of Tennessee, and under his guidance with the assistance of other members, among them Charles McClung, General James White, Andrew Jackson, General James Robertson and Archibald Roane, was framed the first constitution of the State. The Bill of Rights, at the instance of Governor Blount, declared the inalienable right of the citizens of Tennessee to the free navigation of the Mississippi river. The adherents to the newly formed Federalist party opposed the admission of Tennessee into the Union, as they had proposed to grant to Spain for a term of years the exclusive right to the Mississippi in return for Atlantic commerce. Governor Blount, Colonel Robertson, and others who had been Federalists had become alientated by the hostile attitude of their party leaders and joined the more friendly Republican Party. For years Governor Blount had foreseen and advocated the necessity of controlling the Mississippi but the New England and Eastern merchants and speculators were anathema to his settled convictions. A recent pamphlet of the Governor William Blount Mansion Association of Knoxville, Tennessee, gives credit almost entirely to his efforts and those of his brother Willie Blount and Hugh Lawson White, his territorial secretaries, that Tennessee was admitted as the sixteenth state. In the first election under the new constitution he was made Senator, Andrew Jackson was elected a representative in Congress, and John Sevier was elected governor of the new state.[28]

William Blount was in the Senate only a short while. His mind was intent upon the on-coming presidential election. Senator Blount espoused the candidacy of Thomas Jefferson. He and other leaders in Tennessee had been staunch Federalists. However, they had now changed. The hostile attitude of the East and particularly the New Englanders, most of whom were anti-expansionists, their suggestion of closing the Mississippi for a limited time in furtherance of some of their treaty-trading in Europe, their fight against the admission of Tennessee into the Union as a state, and their general attitude towards the people across the mountains had caused Governor Blount to distrust the Federalist party. The New Englanders rightly feared that expansion would lessen Puritan prestige. Governor Blount disliked the Adams following even in the Continental Congress. On September 27, 1796, he wrote to Governor Sevier of Tennessee, telling him "it will be to the true interest of Tennessee in particular and the Union in general to promote the interests of Jefferson and Burr for President and Vice-President." Tennessee cast her first presidential vote for Jefferson. These Tennesseans were opposed to being "sold down the river" by the timid policies of the anti-expansionists, many of whom looked upon Tennesseans as orphans, or illegitimates, and thought that the United States should terminate at the Appalachians.[29]

At this time the whole country was stirred by the European wars. Free navigation of the Mississippi and the "Spanish Question" had occupied the minds of the Continental Congress from the beginning of the American Revolution. Tennessee, in particular, was fearful of losing her "inalienable right" to the free navigation of the Mississippi. As above related, Governor Blount had caused such an expression to be engrafted upon the state constitution. Having become embroiled in the Napoleonic wars, dangers from both sides of the Atlantic forced Spain to the terms of the San Lorenzo Treaty, (Oct. 27, 1795), usually called the Pinckney Treaty. It recognized the long-standing claim to free navigation of the Mississippi. Each party also agreed to restrain the Indians within its borders from interference with the subjects or citizens of the other power. The Jay Treaty with Great Britain and the Pinckney Treaty with Spain apparently stabilized relations with these two countries. Under the definitive treaty of peace of September 3, 1783, between Great Britain and the United States, England had agreed that navigation on the Mississippi should remain open to both of them; but the United States was in open warfare with France during the Adams administration.[30]

France felt that the Jay Treaty evidenced pro-British leanings on the part of the United States and thereafter the United States continually was subjected to the insufferable arrogance of France. Our minister, old "Millions for defense, Sir, but not one cent for tribute" General Charles Cotesworth Pinckney, had been expelled from France in 1796, and was there again in 1798, on another mission, when France undertook to extort money from the United States. It was reliably reported that Spain had joined France in the war against England and that France was to get the Spanish domains in the Mississippi valley. It was known that this would result in closing the Mississippi to navigation. Then, too, Napoleon was ambitious to reestablish a French colonial empire in America. His dire need of funds to invade England saved Louisiana for America. It readily may be seen in what a disturbed state were the minds of the border people who had received little consideration from the Government and whose self reliance led them to feel that they were competent to take care of themselves.[31]

In spite of all of these disturbances, Spain was engaging in considerable double dealings with France and the United States. She was offering great inducements to the frontiersmen to purchase the lands across the Mississippi for colonizing purposes and some of these lands were so bought, though Senator Blount and others were thoroughly familiar with Spain's lofty faithlessness.[32]

Governor Blount championed the idea of moving the Indians

across the river, with their consent and without expense to the Government, as he thought the wilderness country would be more congenial to their native instincts. He also thought removal of the Indians would be beneficial to the development of Tennessee.[33]

With all of these disturbances in his mind, Senator Blount and his constituents preferred the peace and profit that would flow from having the British as neighbors. He wrote an injudicious and unfortunate letter to an Indian interpreter, James Carey, with some suggestion that a movement might be projected to have the Indians aid the British in wresting the lands from Spain.[34] This letter got into the hands of the partisan anti-expansion administration of the Federalists and produced an outburst of temper. Senator Blount was abruptly expelled from the Senate with questionable proof to justify such hasty action; and, in reverse, was afterwards impeached by the House of Representatives on a charge of treason and sedition in having plotted to aid Great Britain against Spain.[34] He was never tried or convicted and these impeachment proceedings were dismissed by the presiding officer, Vice-President Jefferson. Doubtless Senator Blount was putting some irons in the fire, should it become necessary for these sturdy borderers to protect their neglected rights as they long had been accustomed to do. It never has been definitely determined just how far Senator Blount went with the project and there doubtless always will be some unsolved mysteries connected with the enterprise.

His brother and territorial secretary, Governor Willie Blount, who knew much more about these matters than anyone, in a vindication which he wrote for Senator Blount's children, said that the once conceived but never attempted project of getting Spanish lands into the hands of the English was dropped when Senator Blount discovered the overlooked treaty provision against stirring up the Indian tribes. Governor Willie Blount further said: "I, knowing his innocence and pure motives, should never have mentioned these particulars were it not that I am the only person living to whom all of the facts and circumstances relating to the above-mentioned once conceived but never attempted project was ever communicated by the projector." There is no record that he had any communication with any of his constituents about projecting an invasion of Louisiana.[35] M. H. Stephens, who was a lawyer of Memphis and Los Angeles and who married Senator William Blount's granddaughter, says in a sketch of him, quoting General Wright his biographer, that Senator Blount's error, if it was one, consisted in attempting to do by a sectional or geographical coup de main what the government would have been compelled to do sooner or later by force, if a change in the policy of the French nation had not made a settlement possible by the purchase of Louisiana and the sale of it to the United States. Dr. Hugh Williamson, Senator Blount's friend and collaborator in the Constitutional Convention of 1787, then a resident of New York, wrote to Colonel Thomas Blount, another brother, that Senator Blount's motives were truly patriotic. Governor Willie Blount and Dr. Hugh Williamson were as close to Senator Blount as any other prominent men of that day and both were trustworthy men.[36]

Theodore Roosevelt, in his *Winning of the West* dismissed the expulsion proceedings with a few words. He was profuse in his praise of Governor Blount's execution of his office as territorial governor; however he said that he could not defend this last act of Governor Blount. He further said: "They (the Tennesseeans) greeted him with enthusiasm and elected him to high office and he lived among them the remainder of his days, honored and respected. Nevertheless, his conduct in this instance was indefensible. It was an unfortunate interlude in an otherwise honorable and useful public career." This was nearly a hundred years after the event and even now the final answer has not been determined. Justice Story said that Senator Blount was not guilty of any statutable offense. His brother's vindication, which has just recently turned up, though it is mentioned and commented upon by the historian Ramsey, throws some light on the subject.[37] Neither has Governor Blount escaped the scalpel of some of the cynical debunkers who usually see red in every constructive development. He had trod a difficult path trying to keep the Mississippi open, settling internal disputes among the bold buckskin boys, appeasing the Indians, making a state out of the wilderness, and getting along with an unsympathetic general government. He had no doubt become utterly exasperated by the new shocks of hostile foreign empire building in his neighborhood and no doubt was longing for peace, which he sought in the best way he thought it could be secured.

When trial under the impeachment proceedings began in the Senate, James A. Bayard of Delaware represented the prosecution and Senator Blount's convention colleague, Jared Ingersoll, a celebrated Philadelphia lawyer, and A. J. Dallas, the father of the future Vice-President, represented the defense. Senator Blount did not appear. The Senate determined by a vote of 15 to 11, with Vice-President Thomas Jefferson in the chair, that "The matter alleged in the plea of the defendant is sufficient in law to show that this Court ought not to hold Jurisdiction of the said Impeachment and that the said Impeachment is dismissed."[38] This did not end the disturbing situation.

In 1802, Thomas Jefferson wrote Livingston, minister to France, that if France should take the Spanish territory under the San Ildefonso Treaty (Oct. 1, 1800) then the United States must become allies of England and antagonists of France—". . . we must marry ourselves to the British fleet and nation."[39] There was great excitement in the country. It would seem that Senator Blount was a pioneer in his intense desire to control the Mississippi outlet and to move the Indians across the river. Soon after the Convention of 1800 between the United States and France, formulated by Colonel William R. Davie and the other American envoys, France acquired the territory from Spain and the United States immediately bought it from France, neither of them being particular about treatises with Spain. Spain openly protested. Her dispute with the United States did not subside until 1821.[40]

Senator Blount's constituents did not view the "interlude," as did President Theodore Roosevelt. They had become inflamed by national neglect and knew nothing and cared less about breach of international treaties. In them there was a good deal of the independence of David Crockett who, when he attributed his Congressional defeat to President Andrew Jackson, sent this message to the President of the United States: "You can go to hell: I'm going to Texas."

His constituents applauded Senator Blount vigorously as their benefactor and friend. Whether or not there was any disloyalty on the part of Senator Blount to the United States, as the hostile anti-expansionist administration of President Adams contended, it was entirely submerged by the loyalty of Tennessee to him. When he returned home Senator Blount was escorted by a triumphal procession. *Corbett's Porcupine*, a celebrated political journal of the day, almost always antagonistic to the Blount regime, carried an article stating that his reception was a just tribute of a grateful people to the father, friend, and protector of the State. Another contemporary newspaper stated that "his influence in the State was overwhelming and that, far from being shunned, he was received in triumph, as if in defiance of the Federal Government." It was impossible to arrest him. The sergeant-at-arms of the Senate, sent with a subpoena to summon him to Washington, was courteously received by Senator Blount who politely declined to accompany him. He found that Senator Blount was in the hands of his friends. It was impossible to find a local officer who would serve a warrant on Senator Blount. The House of Representatives which impeached him later voted 69 to 11 against compelling his attendance before the Senate for trial. General James White, the old pioneer and patriot of the Tennessee Country, father of

Senator Hugh Lawson White, and owner of most of the land around Knoxville, immediately resigned as Speaker of the Tennessee Senate. They put Senator Blount in his place before termination of the impeachment proceedings, under which the Senator was never convicted. In this way Tennessee rebuked the action of the United States Senate by receiving him with open arms. They would have elected him Governor of the State, it is said, as they did his brother, Willie Blount, had he not met an early death.[41]

That he was a man of engaging and forceful personality seems not to be doubted. Theodore Roosevelt in the *Winning of the West* says that Blount was the first man of leadership in the west who was really of Cavalier ancestry; that he was good-looking, well bred, and cultivated in his tastes; and that he was a man of force and energy, knowing well how to get on with the backwoodsmen, soon becoming popular with them and a man of great influence for good. Roosevelt further says that in a situation that could well have bewildered anyone, Blount steadfastly followed his course, trying to inculcate a feeling of loyalty and respect for the government among these frontiersmen. Contrary to the majority of frontier officials, his influence could always be counted on for good order and love of the Union among those more or less unruly backwoodsmen.[42]

The distinguished Tennessee historian, Dr. Ramsey, says he was "remarkable for great address, courtly manners, benignant feelings and a most commanding presence. His urbanity—his personal influence over men of all conditions and ages—and his hospitality unostentatiously but yet elegantly and gracefully extended to all, won the affections and regard of the populace and made him a universal favorite. He was at once the "social companion, the well bred gentleman, and the capable officer."[43] Many others have spoken in like vein of him. Dr. Ernest L. Stockton, President of Cumberland University, Tennessee, in a recent address in New York, quoting Professor Abernethy, remarked that "It would be impossible to find four men who better represent the spirit of American democracy than William Blount, the North Carolina Cavalier; Andrew Jackson, the protege of William Blount; James K. Polk, the Achates of Andrew Jackson; and Andrew Johnson, the Plebeian who followed no man."[44] Professor Abernethy of the department of History of the University of Virginia, also said: "He certainly was one of the greatest single forces in the politics of the Southwest, if not the greatest, and he deserves a larger place in History than that which has been accorded him."[45] Judge Williams in his *Early Travels in the Tennessee Country* says of Governor Blount's famous letter advising the President of Dartmouth College about schools and religious instruction for the Cherokee Indians, that "It aids in explaining Blount's hold upon his neighbors and strongest of all upon those of the highest character." In another letter from the learned gentleman, Moses Fisk, to his old friend Dr. John Wheelock, president of Dartmouth, from which Fisk had graduated and in which he had taught for a number of years before beginning his great educational work in Tennessee, Fisk reports (April 17, 1800) "that Governor Blount has closed his eyes upon all sublunary spheres—many will deplore—he had a winning address and had been very humane to many of the first settlers in this country and seemed to take peculiar pleasure in bringing forward to business and consequence young men of narrow circumstances and good genius." It may be well to recount that Governor Blount, who was a charter trustee, officially conveyed to Fisk an offer of the presidency of the University of North Carolina.[46]

The Blount leadership in Tennessee lasted for years. The leading men in the State remained steadfastly loyal to him, and after his death to his brother, Governor Willie Blount. Years after his death, Tennessee sent his son, William Grainger Blount, to Congress to fill the vacancy caused by the death of his father's friend, Governor John Sevier. His son-in-law, Pleasant M. Miller,

represented the Knoxville district in Congress. In the twentieth
century Honorable Hill McAllister, a descendant of Governor
Willie Blount, has filled the Governor's chair. Justice Wiley
Blount Rutledge, a recent appointee to the Supreme Court of the
United States, also honors his name.[47]

In the fall of 1797, Senator William Blount and General Andrew
Jackson lost heavily in the failure in Philadelphia of Senator
Blount's personal agent and protege, David Allison, who later
died in a debtor's cell. It is said that he owed John Gray Blount
some $200,000.00 and that he all but broke Andrew Jackson. Loss
of national prestige and Allison's failure must have hastened
Governor Blount's death.

William Blount passed away in Knoxville on the 21st day of
March, 1800, after a brief illness, at the age of 51, "lamented by a
community which revered him with filial affection."[48] There are
counties and towns all over the South named for William Blount.
In his adopted State, Blountville and Blount County honor his
memory and Maryville and Grainger County honor his wife, Mary
Grainger of Wilmington, North Carolina.

William Blount was rewarded for his constructive services to
his adopted State by the loyalty and affection of a grateful people.

Alexander Martin was a native of New Jersey but he spent about forty years of useful public service in his adopted State. The son of Hugh Martin, a Presbyterian Minister who came from Tyrone, Ireland, he was born at Lebanon in Hunterdon County, New Jersey, about 1738; graduated at the College of New Jersey, afterwards Princeton University, in 1756; and, in 1793, while serving as a United States Senator from North Carolina, received from Princeton the Degree of Doctor of Laws.[1]

On account of the close association of the Scotch-Irish Presbyterians in piedmont North Carolina with Princeton, it was natural for him to select this location as the center of his life's work. About 1760 he settled as a merchant at Salisbury, then the frontier metropolis of North Carolina and the chief town of its principal Scotch-Irish settlements.[2] The *Pennsylvania Gazette* of December 10, 1761, notified Alexander Martin, a merchant of Salisbury, and his brother James Martin of the death of their father in the preceding March.[3] They were his executors. This paper evidently had a considerable circulation among the settlers from Pennsylvania in the Old North State. These hardy Scotch-Irish people sought a rude transplanting in the wilderness rather than suffer restrictions upon the ideas of civil and religious liberty for which they had been in violent conflict both with nature and with man for some six centuries.[4] Alexander Martin, by birth and training, was well suited to his adopted surroundings, though he had a much more conciliatory disposition than the average Scotch-Irish Presbyterian. He has been classed as an Episcopalian, as was his younger brother, Reverend Thomas Martin, who was an Episcopal minister in Virginia and who lived for a while as a tutor in the home of young James Madison.[5]

Mr. Madison's earliest preserved letter was addressed from Nassau Hall to Reverend Thomas Martin, his former tutor, August 10, 1769.[6] Indeed the early connection between these members of the Federal Convention was intimate. It is said that Alexander Martin, while on his way to New Jersey to visit his

ALEXANDER MARTIN
1740-1807

mother, stopped at the home of James Madison and brought to a decision the entrance of young James at Princeton. He and his brother Thomas accompanied young James to Nassau Hall.[7] Reports have indicated that both of these brothers were Anglicans. It is known that Alexander Martin was a defender of the dissenters, to whom Mr. Madison made little objection. He certainly settled in a nest of them. Thomas brought his mother to Virginia where he died in 1770. The mother thereafter moved to North Carolina and lived at the home of her son Alexander Martin, until her death at a very old age, passing away a few days after her son's demise.[8] Another brother, James, came to North Carolina and joined Alexander, in 1774, in what was then Guilford County. This brother became distinguished as a Colonel during the Revolution and was engaged in many encounters, winning for himself a name as a daring, brave, and faithful officer. He was second in Command in General Rutherford's Expedition against the Indians in 1776 and was also distinguished at Guilford Court House and elsewhere. After the War he saw legislative service, was on the Commission that located the seat of North Carolina government, where a principal street bears his name, and, it is said, first proposed the name "Raleigh" as a suitable one for the Capital City. He died in his 94th year, in 1834.[9] Unlike his brother, Alexander, he married and left descendants who have graced the State with their name. So much for the Governor's family ties.

The bent of Alexander Martin's mind for public service appeared early in his career. In 1764 the Council of State situated at Brunswick made him a member of the "Commission of Peace" for Rowan County, then covering a large part of the western country and extending to the "South Seas," as the Act creating the County presumptuously provided.[10] Justice Martin was a member of the court composed of Justices of the Peace of Rowan County. The minutes of the court carry his signature, indicating his careful and methodical habits, and record an entry of the Sheriff where, as ordered, he had hanged a negro of the Brevard family named "Dick."[11] This court exercised wide authority. When the town of Salisbury was incorporated by the legislature in 1770, though it had been established as early as 1753, Martin was named in the Act as one of the town commissioners.[12] Public employment was clearly more congenial to his engaging personality than mercantile pursuits and he soon entered the legal profession as an avenue to the realization of his ambitions.

The minutes of the Rowan County court for 1775 record his appearance before it as an Attorney at Law. In 1776 he qualified as Deputy King's Attorney. By appointment of the Colonial Assembly, he presided in 1774 and 1775 at Salisbury over the Court of "Oyer, Terminer, and General Jail Delivery" for the Salisbury District, made up of Rowan, Anson, Mecklenburg, Tryon, Surry, and Guilford counties. He was holding the term of this criminal court at Salisbury on the first day of June, 1775, when Captain Jack is said to have appeared on his way to the Continental Congress at Philadelphia with news of the Mecklenburg "Declaration of Independence."[13] Even before this, in 1770, he was in attendance upon the courts of Hillsboro and was among those lawyers and county officials the Regulators flogged, when they violently supplanted orderly court procedure with mob rule.[14]

The Colonial Records of the State contain frequent mention of his correspondence with the Governor over the trouble with the Regulators. In March, 1771, when the court was due to convene at Salisbury, four or five hundred Regulators were encamped near the town ready to take charge of the court, as they contemptuously had done at Hillsboro in 1770. Although the Rowan and a part of the Mecklenburg militia in considerable numbers were stationed nearby, the court judiciously failed to convene.[15] The county officers and the lawyers, against whom the Regulators were mainly aiming their attacks, agreed with them to arbitrate their differences in order to avoid a bloody conflict. To this end, Alexander Martin and John Frohock, one of the most prominent of the county officers in the Salisbury District, wrote their famous letter to Governor Tryon; but the Governor, jealous of his authority, spurned compromising his ideas of orderly procedure by yielding to mob rule.[16] After the disgraceful affair at Hillsboro, the Governor had crossed the Rubicon and determined to put down riot rule by marching against the Regulators with the armed forces of his office. They met at Alamance, where Governor Tryon's forces defeated the Regulators, and executed seven of their leaders. Alexander Martin, in company with Dr. David Caldwell, was at the battle, still trying to avoid a conflict between the Regulators and the Colonial authorities, though no doubt he suppressed keen feelings of resentment over the treatment administered to him and other prominent men at Hillsboro by these unruly "Sons of Liberty," as they sometimes called themselves.[17]

He was quite active before the earliest Committee of Safety in North Carolina, sitting at Salisbury, and led the escorting party that carried John Dunn and Benjamin Booth, prominent citizens, to Charlotte, Camden, and Charleston to imprisonment without a hearing for anti-patriotic tendencies. For this he was thanked by the Committee of Safety on August 1, 1775. Conditions in the colony made military life a necessary stepping stone to political preferment so Alexander Martin soon became engaged in military pursuit. The Congress at Hillsboro, in 1775, appointed him lieutenant colonel of the second regiment of state troops. This brought him into conflict with the Scovellites, or Tories, in South Carolina in December 1775, where he suffered many hardships on account of the heavy snowstorms of that severe winter. Similar Tory uprisings in and around Cross Creek and Moore's Creek Bridge engaged his attention. When the conflict deepened, he entered the Continental service.[18]

The Congress at Halifax, in 1776, appointed Alexander Martin lieutenant colonel in the Continental Line, and later made him colonel to succeed Howe on the latter's elevation to the rank of brigadier general. In June, 1776, when the British were repulsed at

Charleston, he commanded one of the North Carolina regiments which was highly praised by the commander in chief, General Charles Lee, for its part in this brillant achievement.[19] At Brandywine Colonel Martin was close by General Lafayette when he was wounded, and was also with his chief, General Francis Nash, when Nash was mortally wounded at Germantown. He participated in the gallant defense at Chadd's Ford. An irresponsible slanderer reported him as hiding in a log at Germantown, but his great popularity among a militant people dispelled such slanderous gossip, common at the time against superior officers. Colonel Martin demanded a court martial to examine his conduct at Germantown and was entirely exonerated by this court of any unmilitary-like behavior.[20] However, he resigned his commission as colonel, on November 22, 1777, and returned to his adopted State; but the popularity of that title was and is hard to eradicate and some of his friends applied it to him to the end of his days. After his return home he was placed on the Board of War. This War Council had become necessary because of the confusion resulting from the capture of South Carolina by the British and the disastrous defeat of the patriot forces at Camden Court House. Col. Martin was elected president of this Board of War, on which his collaborators were Archibald Maclaine, Thomas Polk, John Penn and Oroondates Davis. He, Governor Abner Nash, General Richard Caswell, and General Allen Jones were members of the Council Extraordinary which succeeded the Board of War. The Council took over the powers of the Governor and exercised almost unlimited authority when the people became demoralized as fugitives rushed into the state following the Battle of Camden and the subjugation of South Carolina. That these committees prepared to meet the British advance and started Cornwallis's downfall are matters of history. If anything else is necessary to overcome the slurs upon Col. Alexander Martin's military record, mention might be made of the fact that he was elected an honorary member of the North Carolina Branch of the Society of the

Cincinnati as a tribute to his services in the Continental Line.[21]

Colonel Martin, however, preferred civil to military life and like most of the important men of his day realized the necessity and importance of being a landed proprietor. He early purchased considerable property in Salisbury and in 1761 entered a large tract of land in the upper part of Rowan County on Dan River. He also possessed lands in and around Guilford Court House, subsequently called Martinville in his honor after this town was established on lands in which he was interested.[22] He was very successful in all of his business ventures so that he soon became one of the largest land owners in his section of the colony. In 1772, after the formation of Guilford County in 1770, he moved to that county and began his long period of service in the legislative and executive branches of the government.[23]

He became successively a Representative of the Assembly from Guilford County, in 1773–1774; a Representative in the Provincial Congresses held at New Bern and Hillsboro, in 1775; a state senator from Guilford from 1778 to 1782, serving as Speaker of that body for three successive years, in 1780, 1781, and 1782; and Senator again from Guilford County, in 1787 and 1788, when, as usual, he was unanimously elected Speaker of the Senate. His commanding presence, self-possession, and even temper well fitted him to preside over a deliberative body like the Senate and the choice of him for the position, when once made, was uninterruptedly followed at every succeeding term in which the "great pacificator" served. His last public service was as Senator in 1804 and 1805 from Rockingham County, where, on his plantation which was called Danbury, at the confluence of Jacob's Creek and Dan River, he had moved his residence about 1789. In his capacity as Speaker of the Senate in 1781, when Governor Burke was captured by David Fanning and imprisoned, Martin acted as Governor *pro-tem* and continued as such from October 1781 until February 1782, when Governor Burke made his escape and resumed the reins of government. While Speaker of the Senate, during those trying years he attended sessions of the Legislature which met in Salem. He accompanied ex-Governor Caswell to the session held on February 10, 1781, and Governor Thomas Burke to the one in January, 1782.[24]

Alexander Martin was elected governor on the 22nd of February, 1782, on the first ballot, from a field which included such outstanding public men as Samuel Johnston, William Sharpe, and John Williams. He was again elected on April 20, 1783, receiving 66 votes, while his nearest competitor, Richard Caswell, had 49. Governor Caswell said that the Edenton and Halifax men voted for Governor Martin, claiming that Caswell had crammed him down their throats in 1782 and that they were determined to keep him there. Of course, the Western men and the Cape Fear men voted for him, the latter hoping by joining with the western men to establish the seat of government at Cross Creek, or Fayetteville as the locality was afterwards called. In 1784, he was re-elected governor without opposition. As the law then made him ineligible to re-election, he was succeeded by Richard Caswell, who was elected over Abner Nash. His election as Governor again for three terms, beginning in 1789, established a record for holding this high office which has been surpassed only by Governor Richard Caswell. The legislature in 1782, at the beginning of his terms as Governor, through its Speaker, commended his ability, firmness, and integrity. When he had completed his terms as Governor, the legislators assured him of their satisfaction with the discharge of his duties over a period of service almost as long as the Constitution permitted.[25]

It can be said truthfully that the terms of his governorship covered a most trying period of the state's history and were administered by him with dignity and fidelity. Few men have ever enjoyed the popularity of this distinguished administrator and statesman. He was an advocate of progressive measures, such as port facilities and a system for establishing schools in the State. Much of his time was consumed in the settlement of debts and money matters generally, including disposition of the Western lands. In the index to our State Records there are five or six references to Governor Martin's activities.

He was the first of our Governors to advocate a system of internal improvements, including building canals and draining swamps. His addresses to the General Assembly continuously showed his zeal for education. "May we call your attention," said he, "to the education of our youth: may seminaries of learning be revived and encouraged where the understanding may be enlightened, the heart amended, and genius cherished, whence the State may draw forth men of abilities to direct her councils and support her Government."[26] Among other services, in furtherance of education, Governor Martin was among the Commissioners, or Directors, of the Hillsboro Academy, Salisbury Academy, the Academy at Kinston, and doubtless others, established during his first terms as governor.[27]

In 1783 the General Assembly of North Carolina, having provided for the establishment of an academy in the wilderness country, now East Tennessee, named it Martin's Academy in honor of the Governor. This academy, sometimes called Doak's Academy, was chartered in 1795 by the Territorial Assembly as Washington College, under which name it has had a useful and honorable life.[28] It is certain that he was always ready to assist Presbyterians in the Piedmont in their eagerness for education with the forces of his office. Four of the leading classical schools in the State were first located in his County of Rowan: Crowfield Academy, Clio Academy, Zion Parnassus Academy, and Dr. Caldwell's Log College.[29]

When the Legislature of North Carolina granted a charter to the University, in 1789, during one of Colonel Alexander Martin's terms as Governor, he was included in the list of Trustees and became president of the Board, on which he served for the rest of his life. Both his ability and his influence as Governor were available in raising funds to erect buildings for the University and to set in motion, under the Constitution, the head of the State's educational system with a Presbyterian minister from Princeton, Dr. Joseph Caldwell, soon to be its President.[30]

His colleague in the Constitutional Convention, Dr. Hugh Williamson, once said that "the great exertions of political wisdom in our late Governor (Martin) while he sat at the helm of our State have so exhausted his fund, that time must be required to enable him again to exert his abilities to the advantages of the nation." Chief Justice Clark said Alexander Martin was the leading influence in North Carolina when he entered the Governor's office. He was repeatedly thanked by the General Assembly for his faithful services.[31]

We are leaving the main road on too many by-paths. The great trouble is that Governor Martin left little or nothing in the way of records to indicate his activities in the Federal Convention which he left the latter part of August on account of urgent business before the courts at Salisbury. He had entered the Convention as one of the first arrivals.[32] He did cooperate with General Pinckney of South Carolina in seeking six instead of five representatives for North Carolina in the House of Representatives, when the Special Committee fixed the smaller number. He desired that ineligibility of representatives be limited to offices created or augumented during their term and objected to the seat of government being at any state capital.[33] Governor Martin was no doubt favorable to the Connecticut Compromise and must have helped to carry North Carolina's decisive vote in the settlement of this momentous question. If he had voted otherwise, with Governor Martin and Spaight opposing and Colonel Davie and Dr. Williamson favoring the compromise, North Carolina would have been deadlocked like Massachusetts and her vote could not have been counted. While attending the Convention he lived at the Indian Queen, Philadelphia's well known and elegant hostelry.[34]

While serving a term in the state senate he voted for the Convention at Hillsboro in July, 1788, to pass upon the Constitution. He was a candidate to represent Guilford but was defeated by his old friend, Dr. David Caldwell, who was an intense anti-Federalist and bitterly opposed the adoption of the Constitution. Francis Nash of Hillsboro, a student of Governor Martin's career, said that the ablest of his state papers was his plea for adoption of the Federal Constitution.[35] He was about to enter another term as Governor when the ratifying Convention was held in Fayetteville and he was outspoken for ratification.

His colleague in the Federal Convention, William Pierce of Georgia, said that Alexander Martin was a man of sense and a good politician; but not skilled in public debate, as he was not a speaker. Some contemporary has characterized him as having "pursued popularity with avidity." In any event he was one of the most successful and useful public officials the state has ever had. Urbanity is one of the main differences between a leader and a boss. When the State of North Carolina changed the unpopular names of Bute, Dobbs, and Tryon Counties, it intentionally left the name of Martin County undisturbed, in compliment to Governor Alexander Martin, though it first honored a Royal Governor.[36]

After serving for 6 terms as governor, once by succession and five times by election,[37] he was, in 1793, elected to the United States Senate after a warm contest. He succeeded Senator Samuel Johnston who was a strong Federalist; Senator Martin has also been so classed, but his convictions were by no means strong. He was an admirer and follower of General Washington and usually supported the Adams administration, though he appears to have announced himself as strongly for state rights and opposed to national encroachments when he campaigned for the Senate. He was consistently for economy in public expenditures. In his early days in the Senate, he introduced resolutions for open door sessions of the Senate and agitated these resolutions into adoption. When the visitors' galleries were completed, it was upon his motion that they opened to the public.

War with England then seemed imminent. Martin, like his

State, was pro-French and preferred neutrality. He also opposed the Jay Treaty and he was otherwise a little out of line with the Adams administration as he opposed a note of appreciation for the President on his handling of foreign affairs. He became disturbed by the insults of France and voted for creation and enlargement of the Navy, for raising an army, and for suspension of intercourse with France. He finally gave his approval to the Alien and Sedition bills. North Carolina disapproved of the Alien and Sedition Acts, which attitude may have caused his defeat for re-election to the Senate. In any event, he was succeeded by his neighbor, Jesse Franklin. His defeat practically ended his political career, though he did represent Rockingham in the state Senate in 1804 and 1805.[38]

With his fine estate and ample means he dispensed an abundant hospitality on the Dan, entertaining among others his friend, President Washington, on Washington's Southern Tour and accompanying him to Salem on June 1, 1791. The President gave him a silver cup properly inscribed. The governor also indulged in a little poetry as a pastime and his admiration for General Francis Nash inspired him to depict his Chief in an Ode on the General's death. This and other attempts were published in the University of North Caroline Magazine. It may be said that he loved polite living and was a man of fine sensibilities.

Governor Martin died, unmarried, on November 2, 1807, on his estate on the Dan River, which he loved so much. He was buried on the banks of the river. A freshet made necessary the removal of his remains so that no one knows the location of his unmarked grave.

In 1787, while Colonel William Richardson Davie was a borough Representative from Halifax, he was elected as one of the original deputies to the Constitutional Convention in Philadelphia. He was one of the youngest members of the Federal Convention. In the Convention, though Colonel Davie was not so talkative as some of the older delegates, or deputies, his talents were admired and his influence was marked, particularly in the greatest crisis with which the Convention was confronted.

He was especially prominent and outspoken in two instances: on representation in the Senate and on representation in the House of Representatives. He was a member of the "Grand Committee" to which the absorbing question of representation in the Senate was referred, after it had all but wrecked the Convention.[1]

We have already referred to the remarks of Colonel Davie on the issue of equal Senate representation[4] and also to his remarks on representation in the House of Representatives, where he contended successfully for counting five slaves as three free persons in making up the 40,000 necessary for one representative.[5]

The debates on this report and on representation generally, even before the above report was made, were exhaustive, sometimes acrimonious, and often very discouraging insofar as progress was concerned.

As heretofore stated, there was debate in the North Carolina delegation itself. The records show that Mr. Spaight voted to the last with the larger states for proportional and not equal Senate representation.[6] The other North Carolina delegates must have favored the report; otherwise a division of two one way and two the other would have thrown out the North Carolina vote, as such division did to the state of Massachusetts. Blount was in New York. Had Colonel Martin been with Spaight the vote would have stood 2 to 2. So we may infer that Colonel Davie, Colonel Martin, and Dr. Williamson were for the Report. Colonel Davie must have

WILLIAM RICHARDSON DAVIE
1758-1810

had an important influence in changing the North Carolina vote. It has been impossible to get any conclusive facts in regard to the vote. No one who knew seems to have made any statement, and those who have made statements sometimes have confused the situation.

At the expense of repetition, it may be said again, that one of the details in the submitted compromise plan was how the slaves should be counted in arriving at proportional representation in the House of Representatives. This part of the report of the Grand Committee was re-referred to another grand Committee of which Dr. Williamson was a member. Counting three-fifths of the slaves in arriving at population had been one of the fixtures in the Revenue Act of 1783, which treated slaves as possessing both the attributes of persons and property.[7] This ratio was adopted in a resolution of the Continental Congress of 1783, of which Colonel Davie's colleague, Dr. Williamson, was a member. It was incorporated in the Virginia Plan as amended; in the New Jersey Plan; and in the above suggested Compromise report, as brought before the Convention.[8] During the discussion in the Convention a division arose between the North and South and debate became very heated. Colonel Davie arose on July 12 and forcefully asserted that some of the gentlemen wished to deprive the Southern states of any share of representation for their blacks. He further said that he was sure North Carolina would never confederate on any terms which did not rate them at least three-fifths and if the Eastern states meant to exclude them altogether, "the business was at an end."[9] His remarks ended the debate.

Mr. Rufus King one of the Massachusetts delegates, in explaining and excusing this feature before the Ratifying Convention in his state said, that "this rule . . . was adopted because it was the language of All America."[10]

Colonel Davie also favored the right of impeachment of the President which he considered an essential security "for the good behavior of the executive" and he spoke on the term of the

President's office and his ineligibility to re-election.[11] He also favored recommitting the clause on House representation, expressing the view that wealth or property should be represented in the second branch and numbers in the first branch.[12]

He left the Convention on August 13 because of pressing business at home, informing Governor Caswell that, as the state was well represented, he felt himself fully at liberty to return. He also expressed his individual views of the Convention to Governor Caswell on June 17, 1787, when he spoke of the slowness of the business of the Convention, the great delicacy and difficulty of the work, and the impediments at every step caused by jealousies and jarring interests. Dr. Hugh Williamson in a letter to Governor Caswell on August 20, 1787, said that Colonel Davie had set out from Philadelphia on the previous Monday, which was very much regretted as his conduct there had induced him to think highly of Davie's abilities and political principles. Mr. William Pierce, a member from Georgia, said: "Mr. Davey is a lawyer of some eminence in his State. He is said to have a good classical education and is a gentleman of considerable literary talent. He was silent in the Convention but his opinion was always respected. Mr. Davey is about 30 years old." He knew very little about him.[13]

When the Hillsboro Convention assembled to consider the proposed Constitution, Colonel Davie was named at the head of a committee to prepare and propose rules and regulations for the Convention. Those who opposed the Constitution were in favor of curtailing debate on it as a means of railroading their determinations through the Convention. Judge James Iredell, the leader of the proponents for the Constitution, and Colonel Davie, his first lieutenant, spoke at length for a sensible consideration of the submitted Constitution, clause by clause, and as Colonel Davie said, they opposed military handling of the situation. Reverend Dr. Caldwell, one of the chief leaders of the opposition, suggested a class-room discussion of a set of maxims of free government proposed by him, which Colonel Davie contended would produce more discussion than the proposed constitution before them for consideration. Reverend Dr. Caldwell's maxims were voted down by a large majority and the Convention proceeded to discuss the instrument before them. At the very outset, Dr. Caldwell wanted to know why the makers of the proposed Constitution set forth in the preamble "We the people" when the framers of it were representing the States which selected them and not the people. This inflamed those who favored the Constitution and Dr. Caldwell's objection was fully answered by the Federalists.[14]

Judge Iredell, Colonel Davie, and Mr. Spaight all replied to the narrow views of Dr. Caldwell. Colonel Davie spoke at length. He said that he was a member of the Federal Convention and that he and others were empowered "to decide upon the most effective means of removing the defects of our Union." In detail he pointed out the defects which caused the assembling of the Federal Convention and stated that no part of their work was to become effective until the whole had received the solemn assent of the people. He added that the Convention in submitting the Constitution referred to the fact that it "was the result of a spirit of amity and of that mutual deference of concessions which the peculiarity of their political situation rendered indispensable." "The same laudable spirit should govern this Convention. What is there in the business that should make us jealous of each other? We are all come hither to serve one common cause of our Country. Let us go about it openly and amicably. There is no necessity for employing underhanded means. Let every objection be made. Let us examine the plan of government submitted to us thoroughly. Let us determine with each other with candor. I am sorry to see so much impatience so early in the business." Colonel Davie was in favor of combatting some prevalent views by distributing correct information. Many of the delegates, patriotic though they were, had difficulty in seeing beyond the bounds of local self-government and sheriff rule, and the proposed form of government with all of its new features confused them. Few of them really had the knowledge or the experience to understand the situation. It was easy to inflame them with misinformation when the warmth of their blood had not subsided since the bitter conflict in which many of them had engaged on the field of battle during the Revolutionary War.[15]

Colonel Davie explained in detail how the submitted plan would overcome the admitted short-comings of the old Confederation, including the distribution of governmental powers between independent legislative, executive, and judicial departments, with the necessary checks and balances. He explained the need for a bicameral legislature, with equal state voting strength in one of the branches, and with one branch elected by the legislatures of the states and the other by the people themselves. It was necessary, he said, that the foundation of the government should be laid on the broad basis of the people, but that the state governments were the pillars upon which the federal government was extended over such an immense territory and that the states were essential to its existence. The old Confederation, said he, derived its sole support from the state legislatures, which, as everyone was convinced, rendered the whole fabric weak and ineffectual. Equality of the states in one branch of the legislature for the protection of the smaller states was the only way in which the jealousies of the states could be reconciled, Davie explained. The smaller of the states would never have concurred unless this check had been given them as a security for their political existence against the powers and encroachments of the greater states.

He told the State Convention of the many difficulties which confronted the Federal Convention, and discussed the necessity of the general government acting directly upon the people. Otherwise military coercion could be invoked against the small states when such action might be impossible as to the larger ones, making implacable enemies of both of them. It was not easy to reconcile the current discord and clashing interests, different as the states were in territory, situation, and economic condition, except by military coercion. No conclusion ever would have been reached had each of the states obstinately insisted upon the necessities of its peculiar local advantages.

Colonel Davie was many times on his feet during the state Convention. He refuted the charges that the new government would bring about an aristocracy. He admitted that there might be some overlapping of executive, legislative, and judicial functions, but he claimed that the results of such blending, would produce checks and balances which would make a workable scheme of government. At length he went into the objections to the treaty-making powers and the merging of executive and legislative functions in treaty handling.

Of the attack upon the judiciary, he said that the union must either have military coercion or judicial determination. Surely, he continued, there should be somewhere a constituted authority for carrying into execution the Constitutional provisions. If laws are not to be carried into execution by the interposition of the judiciary, how is such to be done?

The question of the suggested amendments, or the Bill of Rights, proved to be the worst stumbling block as the submitted form of the Constitution did not include the Bill of Rights. Colonel Davie clearly set forth that the supremacy of the Constitution extended only to the powers which were specifically granted in it, and that amendments to the Constitution could only be made in the method set forth.

> "How can we dictate to one of the most powerful confederations in the world, when we are not a part of it? Four of the most reputable states have adopted the Constitution and have already recommended amendments. If New York refuses adoption, she, Rhode Island, and North Carolina will be the only states out of the union. If these states were added, they could compose a

majority in favor of amendments, and, by some means, cause the others to adopt them. There is no way of getting them except through the two-thirds rule under the Constitution. It will be of no consequence to stand aside and propose. A dictatorial proposal by North Carolina to the confederation, from the outside, would be like a beggarly bankrupt addressing an opulent partnership of merchants, offering to come into the partnership on his own terms. Such holding out for amendments is neither rational nor political as it cannot produce the desired effect. If amendments already proposed are adopted, they can be engrafted upon the Constitution without the aid of North Carolina and then North Carolina will have to come in on the terms of the confederation and not on her own terms.''

It was impossible for Judge Iredell, Colonel Davie, Richard Dobbs Spaight, Archibald Maclaine, General Steele, and other advocates to overcome the opposition which Willie Jones, Rev. Dr. Caldwell, Judge Spencer, and others had aroused. The Convention, by a large majority, voted neither to ratify nor to reject the Constitution, but to propose amendments, many of which had already been suggested by the adopting states, and await results.

The English-born leaders in the Hillsboro Convention, Judge James Iredell and Colonel William Richardson Davie, were delegated by the Convention to arrange for publishing its proceedings. They did so and assumed financial responsibility for the undertaking. Their draft of the debates was read extensively at home and abroad, and furnished one of the best estimates of the great ability not only of Judge Iredell but also of his lieutenants, chief among whom was Colonel Davie. North Carolinians are indebted to them for the inclusion of the North Carolina proceedings in the excellent work of Mr. Elliot on the debates in the ratifying Conventions of the several states. This work shows that North Carolina, or at least some of its Convention members, stood up as well as any of the other states leaders for adoption. Judge Iredell and Colonel Davie also collaborated in preparing a pamphlet on the Constitution and continued their good work for bringing about the final adoption of the Constitution by North Carolina. However it was questionable whether or not her holding out action had any real effect upon the acceptance of the wanted Bill of Rights by the adopting states.[16]

Colonel Davie was active in calling a second Convention at Fayettesville and during all of these campaigns was the outstanding advocate for the Constitution in the middle and west, as was Judge Iredell in the northeast and Archibald Maclaine in the southeast. In the second Convention at Fayettesville, of which Colonel Davie was also a member, Dr. Hugh Williamson offered a resolution to ratify the Constitution which was referred to a committee. When the committee brought in a ratifying resolution, patterned upon the language of Dr. Williamson's resolution, it was adopted on November 21, 1789, upon Colonel Davie's motion, by a vote of 194 to 77. North Carolina was at last a member of the United States of America, under Constitution.[17]

This distinguished patriot, soldier, lawyer, statesman, diplomat, and gentleman was born in the North of England, at Egremont, Cumberland County, on the 20th of June, 1756. He came in his youth with his father, Archibald Davie, to the home of his maternal Uncle, the Reverend William Richardson, for whom he was named, and by whom as generally stated, he was adopted. His uncle and foster-father lived in the Waxhaws, a very interesting settlement of sturdy Scotch Irish Presbyterians, in Anson, now Mecklenburg County, in North Carolina and in Lancaster County in South Carolina.[18]

Around the 1750s Presbyterian Elder ancestors of Andrew Jackson, David Crockett, Andrew Pickens, William H. Crawford, John Caldwell Calhoun, the Polks, Pinckneys, Dunlaps, Ramsays,

Walkups, Alexanders, and others, tired of fleeing from unwelcome oppression, took their stand. They organized the old Waxhaw Presbyterian Church, and swore "to run no more, but, with God's help and their swords, to fight for Liberty." The deed for the Church was recorded in Anson County, North Carolina, where they thought they were located; but later, when the dividing line was determined, the Church was found to be in South Carolina. Tarlton's slaughter in the Waxhaws, scarcely a generation after this settlement, merely marked another fighting epoch in the life of these strife-striken people. They seemed to thrive on the hardships of life. No doubt, after family prayers, border warfare had been the first subject of conversation in young Davie's old Scotch border home, involving rebellion against misrule. This was also true in his new home, which was presided over by Reverend William Richardson, one of the first ministers of the Waxhaw church.[19]

After preliminary training in the character building surroundings of a Presbyterian minister's home, supplemented by outside contacts of a school term at Queens's Museum in Charlotte, his uncle sent him to Nassau Hall, now Princeton, where he graduated with first honors and an A.B. Degree in the Autumn of 1776. With permission of Dr. John Witherspoon, the College president, and Captain William Churchill Houston, the "fighting pedagogue" of Poplar Tent, Mecklenburg, now Cabarrus County, the only full professors at Nassau Hall, he served in his senior year during the summer of 1776 with a gallant band of his fellow students in active warfare in the vicinity of New York.[20] Following graduation he came to Salisbury, North Carolina, and began the study of law.

According to the consensus of authority he began the study of law under Judge Spruce Macay, who had graduated at Princeton in 1775, just a year ahead of Colonel Davie. They must have read law together, under John Dunn, Colonel Waightstill Avery, Judge John Stokes, or some one else. After his campaigns in South

Carolina under General Allen Jones, his future father-in-law, and General Pulaski, he returned to Salisbury and pursued his legal studies. The studies were again interrupted when he organized a cavalry troop and reentered the military service.[21] He was admitted to the practice of law on the 24th day of September 1779, by Judges Samuel Ashe, Samuel Spencer, and John Williams, composing the first Superior Court of law under the new republican form of government. He was designated in the signed license, addressed to the Justices of the Several County Courts of Pleas and Quarter Sessions within the State, as "William Richardson Davie, Esquire, of Rowan County." On September 30, 1779, he was "sworn in" before the Court of Pleas and Quarter Sessions of Montgomery County, to practice before the inferior Courts, and at the October term of the Superior Court of Anson County he was "sworn in" to practice before the Superior Courts of the state. After he became qualified he was sent by the Governor to the courts in the western country, on the Holston River, no doubt more to ascertain the sentiment in that locality than to practice law.[22]

While he was studying law and after he was licensed to practice, he was active in the military campaigns and won great distinction as a soldier. He became one of the chief military leaders in the Piedmont sections of the Carolinas which included the Waxhaws, where young Davie first settled in America. The dashing young officer united the soldierly virtues of General Sumter and General Marion and surpassed both of them in the graces of life. He became the military preceptor of Andrew Jackson, gave young Jackson a pistol, and won his life-long admiration and respect as the ideal soldier and gentleman. "Old Hickory," particularly in his last days at the Hermitage, often referred to Colonel Davie's gallant operations in and around the Waxhaws and Charlotte, North Carolina, as "one of the most brilliant exploits of the Revolutionary War." One writer has said that Colonel Davie slew more men in personal combat than any soldier in the army of the

Revolution. This of course would be difficult to prove. Lord Cornwallis, in his dispatches to Lord George Germain, stated that his trip from Cowan's Ford on the Catawba, where General Davidson was killed, to Trading Ford on the Yadkin, nearly every step of which was located in Rowan and the territory in which Colonel Davie was fighting, was through one of the most rebellious tracts in America. Subsequently during the late seventeen hundreds, Colonel Davie was made a major general. He wrote a book on cavalry tactics and maneuvers which met with great approval. His brilliant military expeditions, distinguished by daring, skill, and successful achievement, rarely have been excelled. They have been fully covered in detail by all of his biographers.[23] When Davie and Davidson counties were divided from Rowan they were honored with the names of these distinguished citizens.

Following the War, about 1783, Colonel Davie married Miss Sarah Jones of Northampton and settled nearby at Halifax, in effect the Capital of the State, for the practice of his profession. While there he became famous all over the state for his eloquence, zeal, and sagacity. An accomplished gentleman "tall and elegant in person and graceful and affable in manner with a mellow voice suited to expression of every passion, and an easy flowing style to convey his thoughts and feelings." Colonel Davie commanded attention in any situation, and was repeatedly honored by his distinguished associates.[24] He enjoyed a large and lucrative practice in the Halifax, New Bern, Wilmington, Edenton, Hillsboro, and Salisbury Districts, following the judges as they rode the Circuits. His wits were measured with James Iredell and Alfred Moore, later Justices of the Supreme Court of the United States; Samuel Johnston, "the most majestic" of our Revolutionary worthies; Francois Xavier Martin, soon to become Chief Justice of Louisiana; John Haywood, said by some to have been our greatest criminal lawyer, afterwards on the Supreme Court bench of Tennessee; William Hooper, signer of the Declaration of

Independence; Richard Henderson, one of the founders of the State of Kentucky; Waightstill Avery, Attorney General of North Carolina; Archibald Henderson, whom Judge Murphey pronounced the most perfect model of a lawyer the Bar had produced; Archibald Maclaine, one of the outstanding leaders for the adoption of the Federal Constitution, and others. Colonel Davie was a painstaking student, diligent in the preparation of his cases, shrewd in finding the main points and successful in handling them. He was equally skillful in civil and criminal practice and his services were universally sought in capital cases. Both Judge Murphey and Senator William A. Graham ranked him among the foremost orators of America in his day.[25]

His ability, courage, and eloquence were put to severe test, when, amid most hostile surroundings and at the expense of his popularity, he was of counsel in defending his old Tory adversary, Colonel Samuel Bryan, at the March term, 1782, of the Superior Court at Salisbury, against a charge of high treason. Bryan was convicted and sentenced to be hanged. Judge Richard Henderson, Colonel William Richardson Davie, and John Kinchen presented an application for pardon to Governor Burke, saying among other things that Bryan's execution would be a reflection on our government. His laywers were successful in securing Colonel Bryan's pardon. Indeed, when there was large litigation in the state, east or west, Colonel Davie was usually in the midst of it.[26]

Another of his celebrated cases was *Bayard v. Singleton* at New Bern, when he helped to develop the doctrine that a written statute must fall when in conflict with fundamental law. This was one of the first officially reported cases in the United States to develop this doctrine, though the same principle had been followed before in the cases of *Holmes v. Walton* in New Jersey and *Trevett v. Weeden* in Rhode Island. In these states, like North Carolina, there was legislative denial of the constitutional right of jury trial.[27] The Bayard case, which was tried before Judges Ashe, Spencer, and Williams at New Bern is reported in Vol. 1 North

Carolina Reports, page 5. There was a precedent for such ruling in cases taken from the colonial courts to the Privy Council in England, but the above were the first cases in our American courts. Colonel Davie was one of the first American lawyers to develop this principle in this country.

In efforts to recover their confiscated property, the refugee loyalists usually employed Colonel Davie, Samuel Johnston, Judge Iredell, and Archibald Maclaine. This is strong evidence of Colonel Davie's outstanding legal acquirements. One of the very ablest Supreme Court justices, Joseph J. Daniel, who studied law under Colonel Davie, ranked him as the best lawyer and the most accomplished man he ever knew.[28] President Washington offered him a United States District Judgeship but he declined it, remarking to a friend that he would like to get rid of "our d____ judges," if he could afford it. No doubt he preferred the glamour of the general practice and the confidence of the large and influential clients who constantly sought his great talent in a day when genius and eloquence, native sense and reason had full play, unrestrained by the confusion of the conflicting case law of the present day.[29]

Perhaps his greatest service to his state was in his advancement of education. He is generally recognized as the father of the University of North Carolina. "I was present," said the learned Judge Murphey, "in the House of Commons when Davie addressed that body for a loan of money to erect a building and although more than thirty years have elapsed, I have the most vivid recollection of the greatness of his manner and the power of his eloquence upon that occasion."[30] The act for the establishment of the University had been drafted by him and its passage, after much opposition, was largely due to his efforts. As a charter Trustee, Colonel Davie worked for the University's support, aided in the choice of its site, the erection of its buildings, the selection of its professors, and the arrangement of its courses. The early students of the University were frequently visited by him, personally examined, and encouraged in the work of the institution. There is a story that while Colonel Davie and his party were seeking a location for the University and were resting under the magnificant tree, since known as the "Davie Poplar," his colored servant announced that nearby he had discovered a cool spring with a bed of fresh mint and risked the suggetion that this place would be a good location for the University.[31] As Grand Master of the Masons, he laid the cornerstone of the Old East Building on October 12, 1793, and of the South Building in 1798. The Trustees, in 1810, honored him with the title, "Father of the University," and the next year caused the University to decorate him with its first LL.D. degree.[32]

In the Winter of 1798, while a member of the legislature, he was elected Governor of North Carolina. When Madison and Jefferson's Virginia-Kentucky Resolutions were adopted and came before the legislature for discussion, he strongly urged the legislature against any favorable action on them. The Alien and Sedition Acts, which brought about the Resolutions, were a Federalist measure providing for the deportation of aliens who posed a threat to the national government. The Resolutions bitterly opposed the Acts. Governor Davie was a Federalist and was opposed to the principles of the Jeffersonian Republicans. In May 1799, while he was Governor, President Adams appointed Governor Davie, Chief Justice Oliver Ellsworth, his old Convention friend, and Patrick Henry, as Envoys to France for the purpose of settling the strained relations then existing between the United States and France. Patrick Henry declined and was succeeded by Mr. William Vans Murray, the Minister to the Netherlands. Like Davie, Murray was distinguished for his learning, his eloquence, and his skill in debate.

The envoys were received with great consideration not only by Talleyrand, the Minister of Exterior Affairs, but also by Napoleon himself. The engaging manners and courtly address of Governor Davie seemed particularly to attract the attention of the representatives of the French Government. Actually Talleyrand and

Governor Davie have been credited with the main work in drafting the treaty which removed the strained relations and indirectly resulted in the acquisition of the Louisiana Territory by France. This opened the way for our purchase of this valuable addition to the United States.[33]

On account of his great ability and commanding influence, the Federalists prevailed upon Governor Davie to oppose Willis Alston, a nephew of Nathaniel Macon who was a Princetonian and the member of Congress from his district. Alston represented the Jeffersonian Republican views which were sweeping the Country. Governor Davie had declined to be a candidate in 1801, when Alston and he were of like mind in politics and Alston was seated. Governor Davie was nothing of a demagogue and was not interested in molding public sentiment by sacrificing principle. He emphasized in his platform that he never had and never would surrender his principles to the opinion of any man, either in or out of power, and that he wished no man to vote for him who was not willing to leave him free to pursue the good of his country to the best of his judgment, without respect either to party men or party views.

Mr. Alston, well versed in flirting with the public and with perhaps as much if not more aristocracy of birth than Davie, accused him of being an aristocrat and of importing into North Carolina French ideas in his manner and dress, along with decorated French articles for his household. It was said of him that he wrote his letters on gilt-edge paper. Governor Davie lacked the back slapping address of the rough and tumble politician and his Federalist principles were on the wane in North Carolina, as elsewhere. Alston doubtless was aided by the great influence of his distinguished uncle, Nathaniel Macon, a member of Congress from an adjoining district, and Willie Jones of his own County, an uncle of Governor Davie's wife. Alston captured the populace, which was strongly Jeffersonian, and retained his seat. This ended Governor Davie's political career at the early age of

46; but it did not change his political principles, in which he exercised a lively interest until his death. In public he bore himself with almost too lofty an air to win the love of the people; but, if to be praised by those who are themselves worthy of praise is most to be desired in life, William Richardson Davie should be ranked among his contemporaries at the very top in both honor and fame.[34]

Through Macon, Jefferson had tried without avail, before this contest to win Colonel Davie, when the Jeffersonian principles were crystallizing into a party. Colonel Davie declined a commission to treat with the Cherokees and other Indian Tribes, but later accepted a commission from Jefferson to negotiate with the Tuscaroras, which finally resulted in the remainder of the tribe leaving North Carolina to provide the last tribe of the Six Nations in New York.[35]

Following the death of his wife, he returned in 1803 to his plantation on the Catawba in South Carolina, not far below the point where it ceases to form the dividing line between his two adopted states and near where he first settled as a youth. He did not give up his North Carolina connections, however, making frequent visits to the State. In a letter to John Haywood, Esquire, of Raleigh, on June 9, 1805, concerning a proposed visit to the University, he spoke of stopping by Salem to enter his daughter, Sarah Jones, in Salem Academy. She became the wife of Honorable William F. DeSaussure, a distinguished United States Senator from South Carolina.[36] On his plantation which he called "Tivoli" he spent his declining years, living in easy retirement, corresponding with his friends and entertaining them. He became interested in raising fine race horses, and improving agricultural methods, in the course of which he organized the South Carolina Agricultural Society, of which he became the first president. He bought a fine race horse, Sir Arthur, at Carter Hall in Virginia, where his colleague Governor Edmund Randolph lived.[37] Colonel Davie died in 1820 at the age of sixty-five and was buried in the

Waxhaw Church Graveyard in Lancaster County, South Carolina. It took seventy-five years to settle his large estate. On his tomb, with other appropriate language, appear these words:[38]

A great man in an age of great men. In life he was admired and beloved by the virtuous and the wise. In death he had silenced calumny and called envy to mourn.

Richard Dobbs Spaight made remarks on more subjects in the Federal Convention than any of the North Carolina delegates, with the exception of Dr. Williamson.[1]

Soon after the Convention assembled, Mr. Spaight, on May 28, made an important addition to the rules of the Convention. He sought more elasticity in debate by suggesting, with later approval, that the Convention not be precluded by its vote from reconsidering any question and that it not be hasty to rescind a decision reached after mature deliberation.[2] On May 30, just five days after the Convention began deliberations, he seconded a motion of Alexander Hamilton to the effect that the right of suffrage in the legislative branch ought to be proportioned to the number of free inhabitants and thus, at the threshold, helped to throw into the camp the bomb which later almost disrupted the Convention.[3] He never changed his views and voted "No" to the end, even after North Carolina switched to the aid of the small states for equal Senate representation and in a five to four decision saved the Convention and the Constitution.[4] However, unlike some others of his fixed views, he signed the Constitution, as he saw in it the only salvation.[5]

He made casual remarks on a number of subjects. He suggested a term of seven years for the Chief Executive.[6] Houston, a native born North Carolinian and a delegate from New Jersey, joined with Spaight to urge reconsideration of the plan to elect the President by presidential electors chosen by the state legislatures. They claimed such method would be too inconvenient and expensive it would necessitate drawing together men from all over the country just to elect a Chief Executive.[7]

Spaight also suggested seven years as the term for senators, later changing to six. Sherman objected on the ground that if the senators did their duty they would be sent back and if not, dismissed.[8] Randolph agreed with Spaight, because "democratic licentiousness" or a lawless government by the people, had proven the need of a firm senate.[9] He suggested ineligibility of

RICHARD DOBBS SPAIGHT
1758-1802

senators to other office during their term.[10] He opposed the Fifth Virginia Resolution for the first branch choosing the members of the second branch (Senate) from persons nominated by the assemblies of the states.[11] He suggested that the state legislatures choose them directly.[12] He also proposed the provision giving the Chief Executive power to fill vacancies during recess of the United States Senate.[13] On the selection of the seat of government, fearing that New York would be chosen, he stated that if Congress could adjourn to a place which it readily could reach in three days, as had been suggested, this would automatically fix the seat of government in New York.[14] On the treaty making powers, he contended that any treaty affecting territorial rights should require two-thirds vote of the senators present.[15] The Hopewell Treaty with the Indians had stirred up a good deal of trouble in North Carolina because it was thought to be an infringement upon her state sovereignty. The treaty brewing with Spain was, in many respects, obnoxious to North Carolina also, because of its effect upon her western lands. As to the navigation laws, he differed with Dr. Williamson and others who wanted a provision requiring a two-thirds vote for passage, claiming that a majority vote was sufficient, because his section could build its own boats.[16] All along there seems to have been a strong feeling in North Carolina about her ability to take care of herself as far as navigation was concerned. There were considerable shipping interests in and about Wilmington, Edenton, and New Bern, North Carolina.

There are some interesting letters in the correspondence of Spaight, written during and after the Convention. Of the letters that were written by the delegates during the Convention, some ninety have been preserved. Of these about twenty-three were written by the delegates from North Carolina.[17] They are concerned mostly with personal affairs - - arrivals and departures, troubles in getting a quorum, expense allowances, local state commercial trades, like selling tobacco, duration of the Convention, social life, lodgings, and the like but some of them contain interesting Convention facts. Most of the letters are easily to be found and many of them are unimportant. It is hoped that some one may tackle the tedious task of making an analytical survey and discussion of them. This author is endeavoring to stress the more important work of the North Carolina delegates.

The delegates were under a rule "that nothing spoken in the House be printed or otherwise published or communicated without leave."[18] Most of them strictly observed this rule, much to the inconvenience of any one digging out North Carolina's activities in the Convention. On July 26, while answering letters of May 20th and June 12th, Governor Caswell wrote to Spaight that the Convention, in his judgment, had done wisely in enjoining secrecy in their members: "Otherwise it would give more room to Bablers and Scribblers to exercise their powers than they can be at liberty to take in their present case."[19]

On August 12, Mr. Spaight wrote to Judge James Iredell that the United States would not likely in the future risk their happiness on the unanimity of the whole, as in the past, and thus prevent the union from rising out of the contemptible situation to which it had been reduced.[20]

The correspondence of the delegates opens up a discussion which has been emphasized by the more or less recent New Deal attack upon the Federal Judiciary System. Mr. Spaight, on August 12, 1787, wrote to Judge James Iredell at New Bern, North Carolina, criticizing the decision in the action of *Bayard v. Singleton* in the highest North Carolina Court, sitting at New Bern. The decision held an act of the North Carolina General Assembly void because it was in conflict with the State Constitution.[21] Mr. Spaight's letter to Judge Iredell seems to have been the only letter from a delegate opposing judicial review.

It will be clarifying to review some of the facts in the debate between Delegate Richard Dobbs Spaight and Judge James Iredell.

They were as follows: Samuel Cornell, a member of the Council of State under the Governor Dobbs Administration, an ancestor of one of the wives of Daniel Webster, and a resident of New Bern, deeded property in the town to his daughter, one of the plaintiffs in the pending action of *Bayard v. Singleton.* Mr. Cornell then left the State, so as to protect his loyalty to Great Britain when the Revolution grew warm. His lands were confiscated under North Carolina acts which also foreclosed prior owners from suing for recovery of their property, requiring the courts to dismiss such suits, on motion, in order to quiet the title of purchasers under the confiscation acts. The fundamental right of trial by jury was denied these loyalists. Plaintiff brought suit to recover the Cornell property so confiscated and sold to the defendant. Governor Abner Nash, of defendant's counsel, moved to dismiss, under the act, at the May term, 1786. After lengthy argument, the Court expressed the wish to have a consultation. At May term, 1787, Mr. Nash's motion to dismiss was resumed and an able and lengthy debate was entered into before the court by Alfred Moore, afterwards a justice of the Supreme Court of the United States, and Abner Nash, for defendant, and by James Iredell, also, afterwards a justice of the Supreme Court of the United States, Samuel Johnston, and William Richardson Davie, for plaintiff. About thirty like suits depended on the outcome. The Court held that the confiscation statutes were in conflict with the constitution which guaranteed trial by jury, and were unconstitutional and void and the motion of defendant's counsel to dismiss was overruled.

While Mr. Spaight disapproved of the North Carolina decision, he said that some check upon the "intemperate and unjust proceedings of our Legislature" was "absolutely necessary to our well being." The Colonies of Great Britain had a way - - by appeal to the Privy Council. England knew how to handle *ultra vires* acts of Chartered Governments overstepping their granted or prohibited powers. Even the King of England could not authorize a

JUDGE JAMES IREDELL
1751-1799

corporation to do an act contrary to its charter, or the laws of the land. *Winthrop v. Lochmere* from Connecticut, modifying the course of inheritance according to the Common law of England, is a celebrated and much discussed American case. It went to the Privy Council in England, on the question as to whether or not the Connecticut legislature had exceeded its powers. The Connecticut act was held to be void.[22] Of course the English procedure was abolished by the independence of the Colonies but the new states soon adopted constitutions of their own and the state courts, at an early period, began to substitute judicial review for Privy Council review. The American cases, since 1772, are collected in 12 Corpus Juris at page 778.

Judge Iredell in his reply to Mr. Spaight showed familiarity with the Colonial practice.[23] He and his associates in the *Bayard v. Singleton* case were very able lawyers. The *Bayard* case (1 North Carolina Reports, 5) is one of the first officially reported American cases, from a state's higher court, and one of the most important, on account of the great ability of the lawyers connected with it. Justice Iredell from the Supreme Court of the United States, in 1798 in the *Calder v. Bull* case (3 Dallas, 386) expressed similar views half a decade before the *Marbury v. Madison* case (1 Cranch, 137) which was always thought to have settled the matter until the New Deal disturbances. Justice Iredell said: "If any Act of Congress, or of the Legislature of a State, violated those constitutional provisions, it is unquestionably void; though, I admit, that as the authority to declare it void is of a delicate and awful nature, the Court will never resort to that authority, but in a clear and urgent case."

The question of judicial review was not foreign to the members of the Constitutional Convention. It was discussed many times and was, time and again, brought to their attention in the leading newspapers during their sessions. Without doubt, it may be inferred that Spaight personally discussed the question with members of the Convention. Article 8 of the Randolph Resolves provided for a council of revision to examine legislative acts.[24] This provision was fully discussed in the early days of the Convention, beginning on June 4. Then Mr. Gerry doubted whether the judiciary should form a part of this council of revision, "as they will have a sufficient check against encroachments upon their own department by their exposition of the laws which involved a power of deciding on their constitutionality." Said he: "In some States the judges had actually set aside laws, as being against the Constitution . . . with general approbation."[25] And Mr. King said that "the judges ought to be able to expound the laws . . . free from the bias of having participated in their formation."[26] On July 21, James Wilson moved "that the Supreme national judiciary should be associated with the executive with revisionary power. The judiciary ought to have an opportunity of remonstrating against projected encroachments on the people as well as on themselves. It has been said that the judges, as expositors of the law, would have an oportunity of defending their Constitutional rights; . . . but this power of the judges does not go far enough."[27] James Madison seconded Judge Wilson and also said, on July 23, that "A law violating a Constitution established by the people themselves would be considered by the judges as null and void." He said: "It would be a novel and dangerous doctrine that a Legislature could change the Constitution under which it held its existence."[28] Mr. Gorham concurred: "All agree that a check on the legislative is necessary."[29]

Speaking of checks on legislation, Luther Martin observed, in the same connection: "And as to the constitutionality of laws, that point will come before the Judges in their official character. In this character, they have a negative on the laws. Join them with the executive (in Council of Revision) and they will have a double negative."[30] Mr. Rutledge said: "The Judges ought never to give their opinion on a law till it comes before them."[31] When the subject was again under discussion, on August 15, John Mercer said that he disapproved of the doctrine that the judges, as expositors of the Constitution, should have authority to declare a law void. He thought laws ought to be well and cautiously made and then be free of controllers. This seems to have been the only direct objection to judicial review. He never denied the existence of the power. John Dickinson was strongly impressed with Mercer's remark: "No such power ought to exist." He was, at the same time, at a loss what expedient to substitute.[32] On August 22, when the Convention was discussing restraints upon the powers of the Congress, it was suggested that, among others, one should be inserted: "that the Legislature shall pass no bill of attainder nor any ex post factor law." There was some opposition. Dr. Williamson of North Carolina stated that such a prohibitory clause was in the Constitution of his State and had done good there, as it might in the Federal Constitution, "because the judges can take hold of it." Charles Warren, an eminent writer on the Constitution, suggests the significance of this remark as showing the understanding of delegates that these restrictions in the Constitution were to be enforced by the national judiciary.[33]

As stated above by Elbridge Gerry, members of the Convention must have been familiar with the state decisions, declaring acts of the legislatures unconstitutional and therefore null and void. On July 18 the *Pennsylvania Packet*, the leading paper in Philadelphia, gave an account of the deicision of the New Hampshire General Court repealing the Ten Pound Act of that state, and thereby justifying the conduct of the court below, which held the act unconstitutional and unjust. Mr. Warren says that this was the fourth time that such action by the state courts had been brought to the attention of the delegates.[34] On June 27 the *Pennsylvania Packet* of Philadelphia reported the case of *Trevett v. Weeden* from Rhode Island, holding unconstitutional and void the paper money statutes of Rhode Island for failing to prove a jury trial. Mr. Warren says that the delegates during June had already twice discussed the power of the Court to hold statutes unconstitutional and were about to discuss it again in the debates over the

Judiciary in July.[35] The delegates probably heard of the decision in the case of *Bayard v. Singleton* from North Carolina, as Spaight was then corresponding with Judge Iredell about it, and no doubt talking with the delegates about it. The *Pennsylvania Packet*, together with the *Maryland Gazette* and the *Virginia Independent*, had detailed accounts of it.[36]

Burton J. Hendrick in *Bulwark of the Republic*, 96, quotes Edward S. Corwin, in his *John Marshall and the Constitution*, 11, as follows:

> "Nor can there be much doubt that the members of the Convention were substantially agreed that the Supreme Court was endowed with the further right to pass upon the Constitutionality of acts of Congress. The available evidence strictly contemporaneous with the framing and ratification of the Constitution shows seventeen of the fifty-five members of the Convention asserting the existence of this prerogative in unmistakable terms and only three using language that can be construed to the contrary. More striking than that, however, is the fact that these seventeen members included nearly three fourths of the leaders of the Convention, four of the five members of the Committee of Detail, which drafted the Constitution of style which gave the Constitution its final form. And these were precisely the members who expressed themselves on all of the interesting and vital subjects before the Convention because they were its statesman and articulate members.''

Judge Iredell must have convinced Spaight of his erroneous views. The delegate had great respect and high regard for Judge Iredell. Or perhaps it was difficult for him to find delegates in sympathy with any other view. In any event he did not pursue the matter further on the floor of the Convention, though he was an able, forceful, and aggressive man and, if he had thought it advisable, he would not have hesitated to raise the question. In the Hillsboro Convention, called to pass on the Federal Constitution, Spaight made the best speech in defense of Federal Judicial power and authority.[37] Nor has any one yet answered Judge Iredell when he said: ". . . when an act is necessarily brought in judgment before them [the Supreme Court] they must, unavoidably, determine one way or another." The Constitution so provided.

In the Report of the Committee of Detail, brought before the Convention on August 6, it was provided that the jurisdiction of the Supreme Court should extend (a) to all cases arising under laws passed by the Legislature of the United States.[38] "The jurisdiction" was afterwards changed to "The Judicial power", so as to include all federal courts.[39] On August 27, while the judicial provisions of this report were still under discussion, Dr. William Samuel Johnson of Connecticut, a distinguished lawyer, made two far-reaching amendments: first, he added the words "in Law and Equity" after the word "cases";[40] secondly, he added the words "this Constitution and the" before the word "laws."[41] This extended the judicial power "to all cases, in Law and Equity, arising under *this Constitution* and the laws, etc." There was no controversy over the enlargement to include "this Constitution." Its meaning was too plain for argument and it was so understood that, if an action should come before the Court involving the Constitution, the Court had power to make a determination of it. This has been the view of most thinking lawyers since the days of Judge Iredell, whose letter to Delegate Spaight antedated the adoption of the Constitution. The New Deal philosophers, backed by the overwhelming votes behind them, could not change this plain language of the Constitution and the decisions made in accordance with it. The Constitution was enacted as the supreme law of the land,[42] to protect just such raids upon it by a loose-thinking majority in power and it should stand, until it is amended in due course by those who made it. It was written by men who were thoughtful enough to anticipate just such raids and to check against them. There are minds which delight in being "mixed up in a maze of metaphysical jargon" over the extent of the power of review, or otherwise; but fortunately, there seem to have been no such minds among those who framed the excellent Federal Constitution.

Though not written by a delegate, Governor Richard Caswell's letter of July 26, 1787, to Richard Dobbs Spaight is worthy of mention.[43] The Governor urged upon Spaight the necessity for a national Parliament, a Supreme Executive, and "an independent judicial department" among other things, "to decide any contest that may happen between the United States and individual States and between one State and another." The author has been unable to find any similar letter written during the Convention. The old general had seen enough war to feel the necessity for having a better way to settle disputes between free, sovereign, and independent states. He wanted an independent judiciary, one of the greatest contributions of the English speaking peoples to government of laws and not of men, under a representative democracy. He disliked a Congressional Commission for such work. North Carolina, like other states, had long since encountered boundary troubles with her neighbors. In colonial times, disputes between the Colonies were referred to the King in Council where the Privy Council in England heard the disputes before determining them and was supposed to decide them according to law, or under due process, which hears before it determines.[44]

When the Articles of Confederation were adopted, provision was made for such disputes to be referred to Commissioners to decide "all disputes and differences between two more States concerning boundary, jurisdiction, or any other cause whatsoever."[45] In case the commissioners failed in their efforts, nothing was left but civil war. There were nearly a dozen such boundary disputes pending when the Constitution was being framed. One of the first to reach the Supreme Court of the United States was

Rhode Island v. Massachusetts. The plaintiff characteristically objected to the jurisdiction of the Court but the decision went to Rhode Island. It has been said that 31 of the 48 States have been involved in such controversies between themselves and several times the United States itself has appeared in similar litigation with one or more of the states of the Union. The reports of the debates on the judicial department are meager.

The subject was doubtless too technical; but, if Madison's notes and the journal of the Convention were more carefully studied, a great deal of modern mists and surmises concerning the powers of the judicial department would be dispelled. North Carolina took little part in the discussion, save on the subject of Governor Caswell's letter.

In the Report of the Committee of Detail, delivered to the Convention by John Rutledge on August 6, the Judiciary Article, being number XI, was considerably changed from the original Randolph plan. The report set forth that the jurisdiction of the Supreme Court should extend "to controversies between two or more States, except such as shall regard territory or jurisdiction."[46] The exception was supposed to protect the sovereignty of the states. It was thought that questions within the exception should come before the Senate and not before the Court, as was provided in Article IX, somewhat similar to Article IX of the Articles of Confederation above mentioned. This judiciary section, or Article XI, came up for discussion on August 24. John Rutledge, afterwards Chief Justice of the United States, moved to strike out the excepting provision for deciding controversies between the states. He said the procedure may have been necessary under the Confederation but that it would be rendered unnecessary by the national Judiciary, which was to be established.[47] Dr. William Samuel Johnson of Connecticut, an LL.D. from Oxford University, seconded the motion and Roger Sherman of Connecticut and Jonathan Dayton of New Jersey concurred, but Dr. Williamson asked for postponement in order to consider

whether it might not be a good provision, in cases where the
Judiciary were interested or too closely connected with the
parties.[48] Nathaniel Gorham of Massachusetts also had doubts
about striking out as he was inclined to think that the old method
would be more satisfactory than to refer such cases to the
Judiciary. Postponement was denied. Then James Wilson of
Pennsylvania urged to strike, as the Judiciary provision was the
better. Wilson prevailed. When the Report of the Committee on
Style and Arrangement was made by Dr. Johnson, on September
12, the section conferring power on the Senate to settle controversies between the states was stricken as was the exception as to
"territory and jurisdiction" in the judicial section. The judicial
power without exception was extended "to controversies between two or more States; between a State and citizens of another
state; between citizens of different States, etc." And the Supreme
Court was given original jurisdiction when a state should be a
party.[49] This is the language which went into the Constitution.
This is what Governor Caswell, in his wisdom, wanted.

Governor Caswell, long-headed old warrior and statesman that
he was, spoke the sentiment of other wise men of that day, when,
on July 1, 1787, he wrote the North Carolina delegates:

> "Your task is arduous, your undertaking is of such
> magnitude as to require Time for Deliberation and Con-
> sideration, and altho I know each Gentleman that sensi-
> bly feel for his own private concerns in being so long
> absent from them, yet the future happiness of the States
> so much depends on the determination of the Convention
> I am convinced your wishes to promote that happiness to
> your Country are such as to induce you to attend to
> completing this business if possible."[50]

After the Convention, in a paragraph of a letter written by
General Washington, dated at Mt. Vernon, May 25, 1788, appears
some crystalization of the best thought of the time, when no one

could be absolutely dogmatic about an untried scheme of government.

> "I am sorry to find by your letter that the State of North Carolina is so much opposed to the proposed government. If a better could be agreed on it might be better to reject this; but without such a prospect, (and I confess none appears to me) policy, I think must recommend the one that is submitted."[51]

William Pierce of Georgia said of his colleague that "Spaight is a worthy man, of some abilities, and fortune. Without possessing a genius to render him brilliant, he is able to discharge any public trust that this country may repose in him. He is about thirty-one years of age." He was only twenty-nine, and the youngest member of the North Carolina delegation.[52]

In the Hillsboro Convention, called to ratify the constitution, Spaight was one of the real leaders for its adoption, ranking next to Judge Iredell and Colonel Davie. He addressed the Convention, with force and effect, nearly a dozen times during its proceedings.[53] In one of his addresses he ably defended the acts of the North Carolina delegation against charges of having exceeded their authority in making a new Constitution instead of revising the Articles of Confederation. He called attention to the defects of the Confederation, the absolute necessity of changing the Articles, and the authority which they had to make such proposals as were contained in the Constitution then before a Convention of the people for consideration.[54]

He answered General Lenoir's objections to the President's power in passing on treaties and Timothy Bloodworth's inquiries about impeachment proceedings. In regard to treaties he stated that it was thought better to put that final power in the hands of the Senators, as was done, because they were the representatives of the States and all of the States would be equal in the consideration of such matters, though it was not considered as a legislative act.[55] This is another good example of the numerous checks and balances that are interspersed throughout the Constitution. Here an executive act must be confirmed by the legislative department. James Galloway complained about North Carolina having only five representatives and contended that the State was entitled to that many without counting the slaves. Spaight replied that some states had made returns to Congress of their population but that North Carolina had not, though it had had sufficient time for doing so. He contended that the number assigned was the best that could be done for three years, or until a national census as suggested by Dr. Williamson could be taken, after which the right apportionment would be made.[56]

Judge Spencer debated with him the power of the general government to raise taxes. Thereupon Judge Spencer was charged by Spaight with acknowledging the inefficiency of requisitions of the general government upon the states during the Revolution, and yet recommending them at this later date.[57]

The limitation of the slave trade to the term of twenty years was, he said, a compromise between the Eastern and the Southern states. South Carolina and Georgia wanted the extension as they felt they needed more slave help which a twenty year extension of the trade would give them.[58] They bedded together with New England who wanted to preserve the traffic in them. Further, he said, as North Carolina had not thought it proper to pass any law prohibiting slave importation, the delegates did not think themselves authorized to contend for an immediate prohibition of it.[59]

Objection was made to the power of Congress to determine the time of choosing electors and electing a president. Spaight explained that in no other way could equality and uniformity be produced, because if the states had this power all of them would likely set separate days and thus make possible time for log rolling and combinations between them. General confusion would ensue.[60] To the objection that the President should not be given the command of the Army and Navy, Spaight replied that the

Congress alone had the power to raise armies and support them, and that the President was impeachable, if he exceeded his authority. He argued that any army could not be directed properly by a numerous body of men; and that, had not a Commander in Chief, with exclusive power in the Revolutionary War, been appointed by the Congress, the independence of America perhaps would not have been established.[61] General Joseph McDowell from the west, where the Scotch-Irish provided most of the opposition to the Constitution, charged that we would be deprived of our sacred rights of trial by jury. Mr. Spaight said that such rights had not been overlooked in the Convention which consumed considerable time on the subject; that a uniform rule for all the states could not be devised in every detail as a number of them, under their rules for equity and admiralty practice, did not use juries; and that, for this reason, it was left to the states to determine in what cases juries should be required. He further said that since trial by jury was in full force in the state courts, North Carolinians had the fullest security.[62] Again, in spite of his former criticism of judicial interference with unconstitutional legislative acts, he vigorously and ably defended the sections of the Constitution providing a federal judiciary, with power to pass on all cases arising under the Constitution.[63]

After Judges Spencer, Ashe, and Williams, whom Spaight continuously attacked, decided the case of *Bayard v. Singleton*, upholding the Constitution, Judge Spencer in the Hillsboro Convention attacked the judiciary provisions of the Federal Constitution. Spaight forcefully answered him, saying that Judge Spencer's argument against the power of the Courts to take cognizance of cases, in law and equity, arising under the Constitution was astonishing and that a government ought to have power to enforce its laws (the Constitution) or else it might as well have no power. His remarks in the Hillsboro Convention were short, to the point, and full of force. They leave a fine impression of the ability of Richard Dobbs Spaight.[64]

The subject of this sketch had an interesting career. He was the first native-born governor of North Carolina, having first seen the light of day on March 25, 1758, at New Bern. He died at New Bern at the early age of 44 on the sixth of September, 1802, after filling in successive stages many of the highest offices within the elective power of his people. He was Aide to General Richard Caswell at twenty; member of the House of Commons at twenty-three, later becoming Speaker; member of the Continental Congress at twenty-five; member of the Constitutional Convention at Philadelphia at twenty-nine; member of the Hillsboro Convention, to ratify the Constitution, at thirty; Governor of the State at thirty-four; and member of the national House of Representatives at forty. At each interval he improved his opportunities for useful service for which he was well equipped by earlier environment and training.[65]

North Carolina has possessed few public men whose immediate forebearers across the water were so distinguished as were those of Richard Dobbs Spaight. His father, Richard Spaight, of an ancient and honorable Irish family, came to North Carolina in 1754 with his great uncle, Sheriff Arthur Dobbs, the illustrious Irishman who was Governor of the Royal Colony of North Carolina from 1756 to 1765. The Dobbs family had long been an outstanding one in Ireland. Arthur Dobbs had filled the office of High Sheriff of Antrim and had been a member of Parliament from Carrickfergus and Surveyor General of Ireland before coming to North Carolina. He also had won distinction as an engineer, author, and promoter of efforts to discover the northwest passage to the Pacific. Richard Spaight, "a very sprightly gay young man," filled many offices of trust in the colony, including paymaster of North Carolina troops under Colonel James Innes. Colonel Innes held high command with Braddock at his memorable defeat in the French and Indian War. The elder Spaight was private secretary to Governor Dobbs, Clerk of the Provincial Council and also a member of it, and Secretary and Treasurer of the Colony under the Crown. Some of these offices were second only to the

Governor in importance. Richard Spaight upon his death, left his son a fine estate.[66]

At the early age of eight or nine, Master Spaight was sent to Ireland where he received his education, completing it at the University of Glasgow. It may be of interest to note that this youth's kinsman, Captain William Spaight of the 65th Royal Regiment, was with the British at Bunker Hill. With all of this seemingly Tory background, young Spaight became a strong Republican and, when he returned home in 1778 after an absence of twelve years abroad, he joined the staff of General Richard Caswell, serving with him and the North Carolina troops at the disastrous battle of Camden Court House. This ended his military career, excepting his service a few years later in the militia as lieutenant colonel of a regiment of artillery.[67]

His state legislative services began almost in his youth, in 1779, as a borough representative of New Bern, and he continued in this capacity through 1781, 1782, and 1783. In 1785 he resumed his seat in the General Assembly as a representative from Craven County, and was elected Speaker of the House of Commons. During this period he showed much interest in education, being selected as a trustee of New Bern Academy and an original trustee of Kinston Academy. Again in 1786 and 1787 Craven County sent him to the General Assembly, where he was active, among other things, in a lottery to raise funds for a poor house in New Bern. This was a popular way to raise money for religious and charitable needs in those days. His services centered in the Committees on privileges and elections, finance, currency, militia, and representation in the Continental Congress. Spaight opposed the Bill to Charter the Dismal Swamp Canal in which George Washington became financially and otherwise interested, because he thought there should be delay for further consideration.[68]

A little later North Carolina was one of the first states, if not the first, generally to affirm the principle of freedom of incorporation for promotion of business enterprises. By an Act passed in 1795, being Chapter 432 of Potter's Revisal, 1821, the state allowed any persons who desired to incorporate themselves for the purpose of building and maintaining canals. Governments were slow to grant to individuals the special privileges, powers, and immunities which corporations usually enjoy, like limited liability, almost unlimited objects upon which to operate, perpetual succession, and the like. Fears were entertained that unchecked monopolies might ensue and become stronger than the government itself. Other American states had allowed individuals to incorporate for certain charitable purposes, but it was the far-sighted policy of North Carolina to extend the principle to organizations for business purposes, under a general statute, though limited to canals. This policy was soon followed elsewhere, in and out of the United States. It was destined, during the following century, to work world wide economic changes in business administration. This is the view of Governor Simeon Eben Baldwin who was also Chief Justice of the Supreme Court of Errors of Connecticut, Professor of Constitutional and Private International Law of Yale University, and President of the American Historical Association, and the American Political Science Association. Chief Justice Baldwin declared one of North Carolina's main priorities is the fact that in 1795 she passed the first general incorporation law for business purposes since the time of the Roman Empire. In their zeal for shipping, our early captains of industry over-estimated the capacity of their harbor facilities and under-estimated the size of the boats that would eventually carry the world's commerce.[68a]

Mr. Spaight was one of those who protested against a resolution in the Legislature excusing Ashe, Spencer, and Williams, the judges whose conduct in the administration of their trust had been under legislative review. There had been bad feeling for sometime between the judges and the lawyers. Led by Archibald Maclaine, a prominent Wilmington lawyer and then a member of the legislature, charges were preferred against the judges accusing them of having suspended the operation of an Act of the General

Assembly, giving illegal judgments, delaying justice by disagreements among themselves, and failing to attend Courts regularly. Both branches of the Assembly met in joint session and appointed Archibald Maclaine, Colonel William R. Davie, Honorable Will Hooper, Richard Dobbs Spaight, John Gray Blount, John Stokes, and John Sitgreaves, these being among the most prominent men in the State, to a special committee to conduct the investigation. This list of distinguished men complimented Richard Dobbs Spaight, despite his youth, by making him chairman. Most of the charges seem to have been trivially supported and the legislature finally complimented the work of the judges. It looks now as though the lawyers got a deserved spanking. There may have been some grounds for the accusations, as Spaight and others protested against the resolution excusing the judges. Into the controversy was drawn the judicial handling of the case of *Bayard v. Singleton*, where it was decided that a written constitution was controlling against a written legislative statute, in case of conflict.[69]

Out of this continuing conflict between the judges and lawyers grew the Act of 1796 initially abrogating the common law authority of judges to comment on the weight and sufficiency of testimony, or to express an opinion on the facts in their instructions to juries. Strangely enough the Act left judges the power to set aside verdicts absolutely when in their opinion the verdicts should be against the greater weight of the evidence. Would it not be more economical and sensible to let them express an opinion on the facts before the jury takes the evidence, as at common law and under the federal practice which has always followed it? Such priority, though followed by many states, is of doubtful credit to North Carolina, when it is traceable in a measure to an unbecoming animosity towards the courts.

Through all these sessions, though quite young, he took a leading part in many of the most important deliberations. He was selected on January 6, 1787, as a delegate to the Philadelphia Convention, to revise the Articles of Confederation. He was a faithful attendant from beginning to end, reaching the Convention at a time when only a few States were represented, and he was the only one of the original North Carolina delegates to sign the Constitution. When Governor Caswell, on April 24th, 1787, sent William Blount's Commission as Governor Caswell's successor by Spaight, Blount replied from New York, on May 28, 1787, that Spaight had arrived in Philadelphia on the 24th instant. Mr. Blount stated that delegates from only six States had arrived and among them were four from North Carolina. The Convention was called for the fourth of May, but the delegates attended this "secret conclave" with much trepidation. Spaight, however, was among the early arrivals.[70]

From 1783 to 1785 he represented his state in the Continental Congress, at Annapolis, Trenton, and New York, where the Congress terminated the circuit of its small town sittings after periodically lacking the necessary membership to continue proceedings. He succeeded his Federal Convention colleague, William Blount, after he had been nominated for membership during 1782 but was defeated. Many things of moment took place during these years. The preliminary phases of the Treaty of Peace were discussed and the Definitive Treaty of Peace was signed, settling the Revolutionary struggles and fixing for each State its Freedom, Sovereignty, and Independence. There was considerable discussion about the restoration of the property of refugees under the treaty terms but North Carolina's representatives were not much in favor of restoring the property of Tories.

"Clouds of public creditors, including the army, are gathering about us and the prospects thicken" wrote Dr. Williamson. Spaight very much wished that North Carolina would honor the requisitions of Congress to meet the impending financial crisis; but the states were lacking in confidence in one another "to cheat equally," and also were lacking in funds to meet the Federal requests. No satisfactory way could be devised to overcome state jealousy and distrust and to raise the state quotas.[71]

The public lands was a live issue. Provisions for the government of these lands were of great moment. Maryland had just recently signed the Articles of Confederation, after holding out for years on account of the large holdings of some of the states. An ordinance for control of what the Government held was passed in 1784, from which a clause prohibiting slavery inserted by Thomas Jefferson was stricken out on motion of Spaight. In the Congress of the Confederation, at this time, Dr. Hugh Williamson, Spaight's colleague, voted against slavery and divided the vote of North Carolina. Subsequently Rufus King of Massachusetts offered a motion for exclusion of slavery in new states to be formed out of the territory. Such a clause was afterwards incorporated in the ordinance for the government of the Northwest Territory, though not so as to the territory south of the River Ohio.

There was a contest between the New Englanders and the Southerners over handling these vacant lands. Each contended for its individual system, the New Englanders for compact township settlements and the Southerners for more individual, indiscriminate abodes. Mr. Grayson, the Southern leader, wrote that the Eastern people had never before enjoyed any idea of any quantity of earth above a hundred acres, but were now for selling in large tracts of thirty thousand acres. The Southerners on the other hand, he said, had never before been able to reduce their imagination so low as to comprehend one hundred acres, but were now for selling the whole territory in lots of one mile square.[73]

Colonel Spaight wrote to Governor Caswell that the ordinance never would meet the end proposed, because the land above the Ohio would be fully settled before the plan could be put into effect and the cost of removing the settlers would be more than the land was worth. Larger holders of western lands were dubious of cessions acts. Both Virginia and North Carolina were in this class. North Carolina ceded and then withdrew the cession and the State of Franklin sprang into being and applied for statehood.

A violent attack was made upon the Society of the Cincinnati.

An effort was made to purge the Congress of members who did not meet the requirements of continued service for not more than three in any six years. Rhode Island came near being ousted until it was discovered that such action would end the Congress for lack of a quorum. Rhode Island's Howell said: "I have been in hot water for six or seven weeks. . . . I have received two written challenges to fight: one from Colonel Mercer of Virginia, and the other from Colonel Spaight of North Carolina."[74]

Mr. Spaight was put on the Committee of States, to sit during the recess of the Congress.[75] He was present when General Washington resigned his Commission as Commander in Chief of the American Forces.[76] He was also on the Finance Committee and a committee to ask the states to consider investing the Congress with the power to regulate trade with foreign nations as well as between the States. After the states went through the Revolution with the makeshift machinery of the Confederation, and were continuing with an unsettled state of affairs, it was becoming apparent that some adjustments would have to be made to get any united action from these free, sovereign, and independent (and jealous) commonwealths.

In 1792, when he was in the General Assembly, he was elected Govenor to succeed Governor Alexander Martin and filled the office for three terms. In 1795 he attended the opening of the University of North Carolina of which he was a charter trustee. Other than his proclamation of neutrality during the impending clashes with France, and some trouble with privateers being fitted out at Wilmington, his terms as governor were uneventful. Probably the first newspaper syndicate was started during his administration, by Abraham Hodge, with publications in New Bern, Edenton, Halifax, and Fayetteville. By the end of the century there were other papers in Wilmington, Hillsboro, Salisbury, Lincolnton, and Raleigh. Another report indicates county fairs were inaugurated in North Carolina during this period, to assemble the inhabitants for the purpose of trading their produce.

It was during his administration that Dr. Hugh Williamson, in 1793, applied to him for access to the state files for information in writing his history of North Carolina.[77]

Also during his term as Governor the first General Assembly met in Raleigh, after this city had been fixed as the "permanent and unalterable seat of government." Theretofore our seat of government had been shifted from place to place, north, south, east, and west, to suit the unsettled nature of the people who seemingly disliked stability. It was also the first time that North Carolina had ever agreed on a native born son to fill the chief magistracy, or any other very important office for that matter. Governor Spaight was defeated in the election for governor in 1787 by Samuel Johnston of the Albemarle section, as the state was not yet ready for his liberal Republicanism, although the seat of government had been located at his home in New Bern, midway between ancient Albemarle to the North and old Clarendon to the South. Colonial Governor Tryon had erected at New Bern the finest vice regal palace in the Western Hemisphere; but this seemed no reason why New Bern should take the capital away from the older sections. A great many people were enraged by this costly edifice. But the northeast and southeast were at last beginning to agree on some things in the old North State when they elected Spaight governor after a century or more of bickering. Now, too, the west was becoming politically important, holding the balance of power between the older sections. The fight shifted between the east and the west and has not subsided, nor yet had it been possible to arrange representation according to population to the satisfaction of these two sections. North Carolinians have been so independent that it has been difficult to effect the continuity which has elevated other states to more important positions in the union of the states. Hero worship, for instance, has never gotten a foothold in North Carolina.[78]

In 1790, when the legislature elected Governor Samuel Johnston and Colonel Benjamin Hawkins the State's first United

States senators, Governor Spaight along with a number of others including William Blount, was in the contest, but he withdrew his name. He was now ill from strenuous work. He traveled for several years in the West Indies and elsewhere but he was never again in robust health.[79]

In 1796, as in 1793, he was one of the electors to cast the state's vote for President and Vice-President and was recognized as the leader of the Jeffersonian Republicans in his section. John Stanly was the leader of the Federalists and there was a strong antagonism between them. Governor Spaight won in the Congressional election of 1798 and served in the 5th and 6th Congresses of the United States, until March 1801, when John Stanly succeeded him. He was a strong supporter of Thomas Jefferson in the Jefferson-Burr contest, and became a loyal adherent of Jefferson's views. In the formative period, when chaos seemed to threaten, he had helped to form a strong government.[80]

In 1801 and 1802, he was a Jeffersonian Republican member of the state Senate. In the heat of the contest for his reelection, he was drawn into an unfortunate duel with John Stanly which resulted in his death.[81]

In 1787 he married Miss Mary Leach; and the people of North Carolina, in 1854, honored his name by elevating their son, Richard Dobbs Spaight, Jr., to the office of Governor of North Carolina. Some years later his grandson, Richard Spaight Donnell, served in the Congress of the United States from the New Bern district. There are no living descendants of his name.

The North Carolina delegate of whom we have the best written record is Hugh Williamson. He was the oldest member of the state delegation and took the most active part on the floor of the Convention. Like all of the North Carolina delegation, with the exception of Blount and Spaight, Dr. Williamson was not a native of North Carolina. he was born in West Nottingham township, Chester County, Pennsylvania, on December 5, 1735, the son of John Williamson, an industrious clothier from Dublin, and his wife, Mary Davison Williamson, from Londonderry. Mrs. Williamson's father, George Davison, brought her to Pennsylvania when quite young. They were plundered before completing their journey by the Pirate Edward Teach, or Blackbeard, sometimes known as "The Scourge of the Spanish Main." Blackbeard had a cache at Bath, the town which was chartered in 1705 as the first incorporated town in North Carolina, and not far from Edenton, where Dr. Williamson later made his home.

At the age of twenty-one after a thorough preparation at the famous school at New London Cross Roads, Chester County, Pennsylvania, under Reverend Francis Alison, sometimes called "the Busby of the Western Hemisphere," and then at the same academy in its new home at Newark, Delaware under Reverend Alexander McDowell, Dr. Williamson graduated with an A.B. degree from the College and Academy of Philadelphia, in 1757 in the first class of that institution. The institution was formed under the leadership of Benjamin Franklin and after successive changes became in 1790 the University of Pennsylvania. He was a tutor from 1756 to 1759 and filled the Chair of Mathematics from 1761 to 1763. An A.M. degree was conferred upon him in 1760. In the meanwhile, he took up the study of theology and was licensed to preach in Connecticut in 1759, joining the Presbytery of Philadelphia, though he was never ordained as a minister. After preaching for two years, he gave up the ministry because of ill health and dislike of current theological disputes, and began the study of medicine. In 1764 these studies were continued at the Universities

HUGH WILLIAMSON
1735-1819

of Edinburgh and London and at the University of Utrecht which conferred upon him the degree of Doctor of Medicine. He practiced medicine with success in Philadelphia. However he was still troubled with his health and was compelled to devote most of his time to literary and philosophical pursuits.

On June 3, 1769, the American Philosophical Society of Philadelphia of which he was a member appointed him on a commission with David Rittenhouse, Dr. John Ewing, and William Smith, Provost of his College, to observe the transit of Venus across the sun's disc, then attracting world-wide attention as a rare phenomenon. His report of the observations of this commission was preserved in volume one of the transactions of the Philosophical Society and was pronounced by the Astronomer Royal of Great Britain to be "excellent and complete." On the 9th of November, 1769 under similar commission, a report was made on observations of the transit of Mercury and means were thus obtained of settling the longitude of Philadelphia and other places. During the same year there was considerable commotion about the migrations of a remarkable comet. Dr. Williamson conceived a theory of his own about the comet and sustained his position under searching examination. In 1770 his observations on climate, particularly in the Middle States, and the effect of climatic changes on the prevailing diseases was published in the transactions of the American Philosophical Society. Thomas Jefferson pronounced this memoir of the Society "A remarkably ingenious, sound, and satisfactory piece of philosophy." While in England in 1775 he became interested with Dr. Franklin and others in making some electrical experiments and published a paper in the *Philosophical Transactions of the Royal Society* on Experiments and Observations on the Gymnotus Electricus, or Electrical Eel. A number of other scientific and philosophical papers were written by him and published in the journals of numerous scientific societies. Having won recognition at home and abroad for his learning he was honored with membership in numerous scientific societies, including the Holland Society of Sciences and the Society of Arts and Sciences of Utrecht. The University of Leyden honored him with an LL.D. degree.

During 1772, he made a successful visit to the West Indies to get subscriptions for the Newark Delaware Academy of which he was a Trustee. In the autumn of 1773 he and Dr. John Ewing, afterwards provost of the University of Pennsylvania, were sent on a similar mission for the Newark Academy to England, Scotland, and Ireland. He sailed from Boston. His boat was delayed in the harbor at the time when the Boston Tea Party enlivened the international situation, on December 6, 1773, giving him an opportunity to meet and converse with such revolutionary leaders as Dr. Joseph Warren, afterwards a major general, James Otis, the Adamses, and other prominent men of Boston. The disturbance in the colonies somewhat thwarted the academy drive, though a subscription from the King was secured.

Being among the first to reach England with news of the abrupt tea unloading in the Boston harbor, he was interviewed by Lord Dartmouth and subjected to examination by the Privy Council on the Tea Party and other colonial affairs. His provoking pamphlet in 1775, addressed to Lord Mansfield, was published in London, being *Animadversions on two speeches delivered by Lord Mansfield in Parliament*, against the colonies. Lord North called in Ralph Izard and Williamson for an interview and credited the Doctor with the first suggestion in his presence that Lord North's policies towards the Colonies would result in Civil War.

In some accounts of Williamson's life it is claimed that he was the unknown person who delivered to Dr. Franklin the letters which Thomas Hutchinson, the Royal Governor of Massachusetts, and others had written to William Whately, Private Secretary of George Grenville, on the discontent in the Colonies. They were sent to Boston by Dr. Franklin on December 2, 1772, and their publication was one of the provoking causes of the tea episode. The rage and subsequent violence created by these derogatory letters resulted in the legislature dispatching a petition to the King to remove the Governor. Dr. Franklin was, in turn, practically ostracized by British Society. He was deprived of his office as head of the Post Office in the Colonies and was denounced before the Privy Council by Lord Wedderburn in a famous philippic against him, reputed to be one of the choice pieces of English literature in the forensic field. It is doubtful if Williamson went to England in 1772. Franklin came into possession of these letters more than a year before Williamson's 1773 trip. Dr. David Hosack[1] who wrote a memoir of Hugh Williamson in 1820 and all of the North Carolina historians who have spoken on the subject have credited him with being the unknown person who put the letters in the hands of Dr. Franklin. He may have carried the already publicized, rage-producing letters back to Franklin when he sailed on prosperous Governor Hancock's boat, December 14, 1773. He was, no doubt, then breathing some of the atmosphere which produced the highly finished signature heading the signers of the Declaration of Independence.

After the versatile doctor heard that the Declaration of Independence had been declared he brought his continental travels to an end, went to France, and embarked from Nantes for the new United States. Off the Delaware coast his boat was attacked by a British Man of War, but an escape was effected in an open boat and he made a safe landing with his valuable papers concerning the impending conflict with England.

A younger brother, Captain John Williamson, was in business in Charleston and the brothers entered into mercantile pursuits having to do with the West Indies trade. Dr. Williamson chartered and loaded a boat for Baltimore but he was forced to put in on the North Carolina coast, as General Howe had blocked the entrance to the Chesapeake. Edenton attracted his attention so he made this flourishing town his home for the practice of his profession and as a base for his trading in the West Indies.

These cosmopolitan surroundings must have been congenial to

the learned Doctor. In the northeastern part of the colony, in "Ancient Albemarle" where was situated the early court of the province, with the old town of Edenton as the center of its life, "there was, in proportion to its population, a greater number of men eminent for ability, virtue, and erudition than in any other part of America."[2] So said Griffith J. McRee, an early graduate of Princeton, in his Life and Correspondence of Judge James Iredell. He might have mentioned the women too, for it was here in 1774 that the women, endorsing the sentiments of the men, led the embargo on tea by forming the famous "Edenton Tea Party." Nearby lived the acknowledged leader of the Revolution in North Carolina, Colonel John Harvey, who belonged to a noted English family, long distinguished in the colony for ability, dignity, and wealth. Several of his ancestors had performed the functions of Colonial Governor, without leaving any bitterness or ill will in their wake. Colonel Harvey proposed and caused to be assembled, on the 25th of August, 1774, in the face of royal opposition, one of the first representative Colonial assemblies to ever meet in America by other than royal authority.

Here in Edenton lived one of the leading merchants in the Continental Congress, Joseph Hewes, whom the Harvey assembly sent to the Continental Congress and whom John Adams credited with determining the vote for independence.[3] He was a signer of the Declaration of Independence, the "work horse" of the Marine Committee, and the friend and patron of Admiral John Paul Jones, familiarly known as "the North Carolina Captain." In this society were Colonel Edward Buncombe, a cultivated, wealthy, and most hospitable gentleman, born in St. Kitts, educated in England, and mortally wounded at Germantown at the head of a regiment which was equipped largely at his own expense; Thomas Jones, an Englishman of the very fist legal rank in genius and learning, and one of the drafters of North Carolina's first constitution; Governor Samuel Johnston of Dundee, Scotland, North Carolina's first United States Senator, a majestic figure, outstanding in ability, learning, wealth, and character, and successor to Colonel John Harvey as the leader of the Whig Party. Governor Johnson even surpassed, as a champion of people's rights, his learned uncle colonial Governor Gabriel Johnston who came to the neighborhood from the elevating atmosphere of a professorship of Oriental Languages at the University of St. Andrews and from close association in England with such leaders as Bolingbroke, Poultney, Sir James Johnston, William Johnston, Earl of Bath, and Spencer Compton, Baron of Wilmington. Governor Samuel Johnston was elected president of the Continental Congress, but declined the honor.

A polite visitor coming into this neighborhood more than likely would have met Sir Nathaniel Dukenfield, breezy, good natured, and popular; Dr. Cathcart and his two daughters who, with their beauty, wit, and wealth, spiced up the society of the entire province; Stephen Cabarrus, a native of France, and an able merchant, with generous feelings and liberal sentiments; Richard Caswell, who, in 1746, age 17, came down from Maryland with a letter of introduction from governor to governor and soon took high rank as deputy surveyor, lawyer, orator, statesman, and soldier. Mr. Caswell filled with distinction many offices from the Assembly to Governor and from militia Colonel to Major General in the field. The visitor would also have met numerous others from different parts of the world, including Colonel John Dawson, the master of hospitable Eden House and the husband of the accomplished daughter of Governor Gabriel Johnston; Charles Johnston, an Englishman of "courage, patriotism, and intelligence;" and John Gray, a Scottish gentleman, who came over in the early 1700's. Thomas Barker, a well known London-born lawyer with Inner Temple training, also lived here with his handsome daughter, Penelope, who headed the Edenton Tea Party. And we must not overlook the most distinguished of them all, Judge James Iredell, of Sussex County, England, who was the ablest lawyer in the colony, not excepting his accomplished rival,

Governor Samuel Johnston, into whose family Judge Iredell married.

Speaking of the very early days of this Albemarle section, Bancroft's remarks are still worthy of quotation: "Here was a colony of men from civilized life, scattered among the forests, resting on the bosom of nature. With absolute freedom of conscience, benevolent reason was the simple rule of their conduct. Are there any who doubt man's capacity for self government, let them study the early history of North Carolina." Edenton was too remote, after the center of the population moved away from the Albemarle, to remain the capital; but the superior wealth, intellect, and culture of her leaders long influenced the life of the province. The Assembly met in Edenton from 1720 to 1738 and again from 1740 to 1743. Hewes, Barker, and Johnston were perhaps the most prominent Burgesses from the town. This brief resume is perhaps the quickest introduction to the community into which Dr. Williamson moved and will at least offer the opportunity of research to any one who may dispute the estimate placed upon its society by McRee and others.

When the war clouds thickened in the South, particularly in the Carolinas, Williamson was offered and accepted the position of Surgeon General of North Carolina troops. After personally assuming heavy financial burdens in equipping his medical corps, he participated with General Caswell and North Carolina troops in the disastrous battle of Camden Court House. Here he performed signal medical service not only for the American troops, among whom was a brother of Andrew Jackson, but also for the British antagonists. Under a flag of truce he got behind the British lines for several months to administer aid to the suffering American prisoners, becoming involved in a controversy with Lord Conrwallis over the practice of inoculating soldiers for smallpox. The British commander did not favor this method of handling the prevalent scourge. Dr. Williamson had already won a reputation in New Bern and elsewhere for similar treatment. His services with the troops in camp at Camden, attending to their diet, sanitation, dress, and lodgings, thus lessening many of the usual ills of the soldier's life, greatly enhanced his reputation for patriotic zeal. On December 1, 1780, he wrote a long letter to Honorable Thomas Benbury, Speaker of the Commons, detailing the conditions in camp after the Camden catastrophe. This letter is still preserved in the State Records.[4]

It was an easy transition for Dr. Williamson from war to politics. Edenton, on the 17th day of April, 1782, selected the accomplished Surgeon General for the General Assembly, following the community's practice of recognizing talent. On May 3, 1782, the General Assembly elected the Doctor a delegate from North Carolina to the Continental Congress, together with Abner Nash, Benjamin Hawkins, and William Blount. Mr. Blount, after serving a year, resigned on April 30, 1783, and resumed his seat in the General Assembly from Craven County. Richard Dobbs Spaight from the same county took his place, so that three of the North Carolina delegates from the eastern part of North Carolina were going through similar training for the work of the Constitutional Convention. In the General Assembly Dr. Williamson at once became active and presented a bill for promotion of learning in the District of Edenton. Though his services in the Assembly were short, due to early promotion to the federal field, he served on many of its most important committees.

Toward the close of the American Revolution, the economic and political well being, local and federal, had all but collapsed. Paper money issued both by the states and the Continental Congress had become almost worthless and the limit for borrowing had been reached. Local and national governments had exhausted themselves exercising their right to issue paper money and negotiate loans. The only means left under the Articles of Confederation for raising funds was to make requisition upon the states for their proportionate part of governmental expenses; but, under Article 8 of the Articles of Confederation, the proportion of each state was fixed on the basis of land values, "granted or surveyed to any person, etc.," and these values were to be ascertained according to such *mode* as the Congress should establish. This wording was too indefinite to be followed with any degree of fairness by the sovereign states, each of which had the final word as to what it should contribute. The thickly populated sections deemed Article 8 unfair to them and the sections with vast areas of waste land were not overly fair in construing "granted or surveyed to any person," using the subterfuge that the lands were still enemy held. Not until after the Jay Treaty were the British entirely driven from their western trading forts and posts. Failing in the use of land as an equalizing basis in reaching the quotas of the several states, Congress turned to population as a measure and then controversy arose about counting slaves; but this was finally overcome by adoption of the subsequently famous three-fifths rule. Five slaves were to count as three persons. The South generally favored this rule.

During the debate on referring the mode of valuation to the states, Mr. Elephalet Dyer of Connecticut, facetiously interpreting the current suspicions, moved a proviso "that each of the States should cheat equally."[5] So reported Jonathan Elliot who edited Madison's Diary of the Debates in the Continental Congress. Robert Morris, at the head of finances, threatened time and again to quit and go home, but his fertile mind and that of Alexander Hamilton and others continued to devise systems of taxation both direct and indirect, to meet the needs of the government. There was the 5% impost which was obnoxious to some of the commercial states, like New York. Over a limited period of time, specific tarrif duties were suggested on some articles and the 5% on others. Such direct taxes as the excise on spirits and the head tax on persons, as well as a tax on land, were favored or fought according to what vicinities were most affected. To equalize the burden that the indirect impost supposedly placed upon them, some of the "landless' states raised the old cry that the states with large holdings of western lands should cede them to the United States for the good of all. Failure to do this was one of the reasons which delayed ratification of the Articles of Confederation. Maryland refused up to the last to ratify because, she contended, all of the colonies had fought to separate the lands from Great Britain and all of them should get benefit therefrom. This running account of the main issues is given to picture in a brief though fragmentary way the field into which the subject of this sketch was entering.

Dr. Williamson, as usual, industriously plied his multifarious duties, being particularly zealous with his colleagues in keeping his state fully aware of happenings in the central government. He wrote the governor that, unless something was done to regulate roads and ferries, the post road from Boston to Savannah would be closed south of Petersburg, where the mail under British management had ridden fortnightly.

In 1783, the Congress was considering the seat of government. Dr. Williamson contended for a Southern location and expressed to the governor his preference for the falls of the Potomac near where Washington is now located. He favored the 5% impost tax as did his state[6] and he also favored the tax upon spirits, though it was very unpopular even in his own district.

A most perplexing problem concerned making adjustment of the war debts of the states with the general government. He first opposed any change in the Articles of Confederation as constituted, fixing the state quotas in accordance with the value of all lands "granted to or surveyed for any person," though the North Carolina delegation finally voted for the change. He realized that keeping the western lands eventually would raise the quota of North Carolina and he favored ceding them to the general government. He considered this a method for paying the national debt, but in such a way as also to protect the unadjusted state debt to the general government and to get some credit for the large sums that North Carolina had already spent for the general good.

He wrote energetically to the Governor about the various methods of raising money, including the 5% duty on imports, the direct
tax of $1.00 on every hundred acres, the imposition of a poll tax,
the excise on spirits, and cession of the western lands.

In the General Assembly, on April 19, 1784, a bill was introduced and finally passed ceding the western lands to the national
government. A bitter fight ensued. Some thought that a spirit of
speculation had been the cause of the legislation, though it had
long been sought as a common back-log to meet obligations of the
central government. After a spirited contest the Cession Act was
repealed in October. Dr. Williamson thought the state had hastily
passed the bill without protecting her best interest. He also
wanted to use the western lands to force some of the states like
Georgia and Rhode Island to acquiesce in other congressional
requests for the common good like the 5% impost. He wrote at
length to the Governor in a letter from Edenton with detailed
criticism of the Cession Act, since referred to as "a State paper of
the highest value."[7] Just a few of his contentions might be helpful.
Williamson argued that the Cession Act had failed to consider the
value of the western lands in the settlement of the state's local
obligations, much of the lands already having been granted to
Revolutionary soldiers for services. He also stressed their value in
properly settling the state's unadjusted debt to the central government. For instance, due credit had not been given for the great
expense to which North Carolina had gone in the Indian expeditions, rightfully, as he thought, a federal responsibility. The
arguments of Dr. Williamson, Colonel Davie, Richard Dobbs
Spaight, and others along the same lines finally brought about
repeal of the Cession Act.

The preamble to the repealing act set forth some of the defects
of the cession. Here it is stated that the cession was made in full
confidence that the whole expense of the Indian Expeditions and
the militia aid to South Carolina and Georgia should be passed to
the account of the state's quota of the Continental expenses

incurred by the War. It added that the belief had been other states holding western lands would make similar cessions, and that all the states would unanimously grant an impost of 5% as a common fund for the discharge of the federal debt. On the contrary Massachusetts and Connecticut, after accepting the cessions of New York and Virginia, had laid claim to a large part of the ceded territory and claimed that the 5% impost measures for building up a common fund to discharge the federal debt either had been frustrated or delayed. A detailed discussion of these controversies already fully reported by all of our leading historians would be too long for this book; suffice it to say, that Dr. Williamson knew the situation perhaps better than any of our representatives and did as much as any one in guiding the state's course to a solution of the difficult situation. Some writers claim that the rising state of Franklin hastened the repeal, but it seems more reasonable to infer that the defects pointed out by Williamson and others brought it about.

Dr. Williamson kept his state informed about the Definitive Treaty of Peace and Commerce with Great Britain, which was not concluded until September 3, 1783, and other trade agreements; about the low state of finances; about the prevalent low estimates of North Carolina's support of the War, which he and William Blount openly and vigorously answered; about the deplorable state of continental money, with coonskins and raw hides, in some localities, supplementing money as mediums of exchange; about the imbecility of Congress in making treaties and then not being able to enforce them; and, about most of the other activities of the Continential Congress between 1782 and 1785.

The General Assembly of North Carolina on May 14,1783, thanked Hugh Williamson and William Blount for their address to the Minister of France on the auspicious birth of the Dauphin of France. The address was favorably received by the Court of France which assured the inhabitants of North Carolina of the particular interest his Christian Majesty would constantly take in their prosperity. This was some evidence of the state's pride in her independent sovereignty and her enjoyment of the flattery that she received from dipping into a little private diplomacy. On May 24, 1784, the General Assembly also expressed the state's appreciation of faithful services to Dr. Hugh Williamson and Benjamin Hawkins.

In 1784, when Thomas Jefferson inserted into his bill a provision prohibiting slavery in the states to be carved out of the western lands, recently acquired by the national government, Richard Dobbs Spaight moved that this provision be stricken out. This was done; but Dr. Williamson voted for its retention, as it met with his views on slavery. Spaight thought that some provision should be included for the protection of owners of slaves who fled into the protected territory.

Before moving on, reference might be made to the opportunities afforded Blount, Spaight, and Williamson for meeting the leading men of the day. This applied especially to Dr. Williamson who served the allowable time of three continuous terms in those ambulatory sessions, sitting successively at Philadelphia, Princeton, Annapolis, Trenton, and new York. Collaborating with him from time to time, in his first federal legislative service, were many later deputies, delegates, and commissioners, to the Constitutional Convention. These included Elbridge Gerry, Nathaniel Gorham, and Rufus King, commissioned as delegates from Massachusetts; Dr. William S. Johnson, Roger Sherman, and Oliver Ellsworth, delegates from Connecticut; Alexander Hamilton, Judge John Lansing, and Gouverneur Morris, delegates from New York; William Churchill Houston, native of Cabarrus County North Carolina but a commissioner from New Jersey; James Wilson, Thomas Mifflin, George Clymer, Thomas Fitzsimmons, and James Wilson, deputies from Pennsylvania; Gunning Bedford, deputy from Delaware; James McHenry, Daniel Carroll, and Luther Martin, deputies from Maryland; James Madison, deputy from Virginia; John Rutledge and Charles Pinckney, deputies from South Carolina; and William Few, Abraham Baldwin, and William Houston, deputies from Georgia. Alexander Hamilton, William Churchill Houston, and James Madison were also commissioners to the Annapolis Convention, as was Dr. Williamson.

The house journal of the General Assembly of North Carolina for the latter part of 1785 shows that the vigorous-minded doctor was again representing Chowan County. His colleague in the Constitutional Convention, Richard Dobbs Spaight, on Dr. Williamson's motion, was unanimously chosen Speaker. Bills for securing the State's literary property and for incorporating religious societies, and the Protestant Episcopal Churches, were sponsored by him. Complaint was made that the soldiers could not be disbanded for want of money to pay them. Dr. Williamson then sponsored bills to settle with the veterans and to provide for widows and orphans of Revolutionary soldiers.

On June 10, 1786, Dr. Williamson was elected one of the commissioners to the Annapolis Convention which had been arranged at Mount Vernon for the purpose of settling the commercial conflicts between the new states. The states had been unable to agree on any plan. Dr. Williamson proceeded to the Convention but arrived just as it was adjourning, not having entered upon the business for which it was assembled. It did, however, suggest the call of the Federal Convention. This Annapolis Convention has already been discussed in the Foreward to these papers.

When North Carolina was notified of the call for the Convention at Philadelphia on May 4, 1787, her General Assembly had already elected five deputies and the Governor was authorized to supply vacancies. Willie Jones, one of the five deputies so commissioned, declined and Governor Caswell, at Kinston, on April 3, 1787, appointed Hugh Williamson, one of the deputies in the place of Willie Jones. Dr. Williamson felt flattered by the appointment and proceeded, in due course, to the performance of his serious duties. He was more talkative in the Convention than any of the North Carolina deputies, untiringly busying himself with the details of almost all of the leading questions that came before the body. Whenever the Convention elected a special committee, composed of a deputy from each state, for considering important questions, he was usually selected to represent North Carolina. The only exception was when Colonel Davie was elected to represent the State on the Grand Committee, to settle the dispute over representation in the legislative branch. Even here, however, Dr. Williamson was elected by the Convention on the Committee to reconsider that part of the Grand Committee's report which consumed proportional representation in the House of Representatives.

When the report on original apportionment of representation in the House came from his committee into the Convention, he opposed reducing New Hampshire from three to two and favored more representatives from Rhode Island and Providence Plantations. In this dispute, he was the first to move a resolution for a national census to be taken on the first year after the new government should organize and periodically thereafter. He thereby advanced the modern view that the representation of the several states might be increased or decreased in accordance with the census returns. North Carolina was the only state whose representation was doubled after the first census.[8]

He served on many other important committees as the representative of North Carolina, and even at the expense of tediousness some of them will be mentioned: on assumption of state debts, to consider the necessity and expediency of the debts of the several states being assumed by the United States, concurring in the idea that, if such debts were to be assumed, unlocated lands of the particular states should be surrendered to the general government; on the slave trade; and on Navigation Acts and commercial regulations, favoring a two-thirds vote of Congress on such acts. North Carolina and Virginia both proposed an amendment to the Constitution to this end, which might have checked some of the present interstate commerce litigation. When the Convention was reaching its close, he was also selected to represent North Carolina on a Special Committee consisting of one member from each state to consider all remaining matters not covered and to make a report to the Convention. From the above cursory review it will be seen that he was not inactive in the Convention. The important business before the Convention was handled by these Committees. It is universally known that Dr. Williamson was an indefatigable worker of undeviating integrity and honor and it reasonably may be inferred, aside from what he said on the floor, that he performed his full duty to the best of his ability.

He made remarks on the following controversial provisions of the Constitution: on more than one executive, a provision preferring three executives rather than one, and that advocated a six year term in case of one executive, with ineligibility to succeed himself; on impeachment; on method of electing the chief executive; on two-thirds legislative vote for overriding a presidential veto; on the number of the Senators, a provision which preferred a small number and such a system as would preserve the existence of the state governments; on Senator's election, pay, and term of office; on veto of state laws, opposing any power that would restrain the states from regulating their internal policies; on basis for representation in the legislative branch, suggesting a compromise and approving commitment of this nagging question to a smaller body which might consider the matter with more coolness. He also debated upon oath of office, contending that oaths should be reciprocal, with state and national officers; on control of money bills, in which regard he complained that the small states had forsaken the condition on which North Carolina had agreed on equality in the Senate, namely, because it was agreed that money bills should be confined to the House of Representatives, in return for equality of votes for the small states in the Senate; on state payment of representatives, which he opposed; on ineligibility of members to any office created by the Congress, stating that he had scarcely seen a single corrupt measure in the legislature of

North Carolina that could not be traced to office-hunting; on prayers in the Convention, observing that the true cause of the omission could not be mistaken—the Convention had no funds; on jury trial in civil cases; on the capitation tax clause; on treaty-making power; on signing the Constitution; on the national capital; on the standing army; on cases between states; on executive succession; on prohibition of state imposts; on western claims; on the vice-president; on paying electors out of the national treasury; and on various other subjects.[9]

Some important provisions in the Constitution were suggested by him. He first recommended the two-thirds vote for overriding the President's veto and the six year term for United States Senators.[10] He and Rufus King of Massachusetts fixed the language in the Constitution which applied to incompatible offices.[11] He suggested that the President be impeachable.[12] He was one of the first to propose voting representation for three-fifths of the slaves, though this was in the Virginia plan as amended, the New Jersey plan, and the Compromise Committee plan. He helped to end this crisis by conceding legislative control of commerce and postponement of the prohibition against slave importation until 1808.[13] He and Col. Davie were the only delegates from North Carolina who were outspoken in the convention on the Connecticut Compromise, which provided for equal representation in the Senate and proportional representation in the House of Representatives. No doubt he aided in switching North Carolina to the small states, giving these states the necessary controlling vote to carry their point and save the Convention and the Constitution. As above stated he was in favor of some kind of compromise and like the small states was always in favor of preserving state sovereignty, as far as it could be practicable. That he was the prime mover for a national census already has been stated, though the importance of this priority will bear repetition. It is said that Dr. Williamson was the first to assert that the Constitution would be the supreme law of the land. This can be substantiated in

Article VI of the Constitution, where the wording states: "This Constitution, and the Laws of the United States which shall be made in pursuance thereof . . . shall be the supreme Law of the Land."[14] National legislative acts are only valid when passed in pursuance of the Constitution.

When he wrote to Governor Caswell on August 20, "how difficult a part had fallen to the share of our State in the course of the business," and said that the delegates would be at liberty at some future time to explain it, he no doubt had in mind the debate in our own delegation and the result of the debate which switched North Carolina's vote from the large to the small states.

In August 1787, just before the close of the Constitutional Convention in Philadelphia, Dr. Williamson published serially in *The American Museum* a number of letters signed "Sylvius," which he had written during the year 1786. A North Carolina contemporary referred to them as the "Essays on Money."[15] These letters were first published in New York in pamphlet form. Recently they have been reproduced by Dr. W. K. Boyd in the publications of the Historical Society of Trinity College. From a rare original pamphlet copy, in the writer's library, it may be seen that they discuss the scarcity of money, the evils of paper currency, national dress, foreign luxuries, the federal debt, public taxes, the advantages of an excise tax over a land and poll tax, and the promotion of domestic manufacturers. Here the reader may find an interesting insight into political and economic conditions in the United States, with considerable information on life in North Carolina during the period. Inside and outside of North Carolina these letters were extensively used by advocates of the Constitution, preliminary to the call of the ratifying Conventions. Their wording indicates that Williamson was the "keynoter" of the Federalists in North Carolina. Though valuable, they have been largely overlooked in histories and pamphlets treating the period which they cover.

While in Philadelphia Dr. Williamson and Governor Alexander

Martin lodged at the old Indian Queen, with other delegates such as Caleb Strong, Elbridge Gerry, and Nathaniel Gorham of Massachusetts; James Madison, George Mason, and Edmund Randolph of Virginia; Charles Pinckney of South Carolina, and Alexander Hamilton of New York. This was a celebrated tavern of that day. It was described by Rev. Manasseh Cutler, a guest from Massachusetts, to have been located on Third Street near the center of the town between Market and Chestnut, where there was a charge of "only 25 Pennsylvania currency a day, including servants and horses, with extras for liquor." Dr. Cutler said that it was kept in an excellent style. His journal gives an interesting account of his reception on his arrival at the tavern, its ample accommodations, the bar, his quarters, the guests, and the general surroundings, as well as the obliging "bell boys" of that day, with their sparkling costumes.[16]

He relates a pleasant visit to Dr. Franklin's home and tells of the Doctor's story about a two-headed snake which he had preserved in a vial and which he was in the act of comparing with the Convention. Dr. Franklin speculated on what would have happened had the two heads of the snake decided to go on opposite sides of the stem of a bush, neither head consenting to come back, nor give way. At this point Franklin's story was cut short by a suggestion of the secrecy of the Convention. It is said that someone constantly had to be kept with the exuberant Doctor to stop him from telling all he knew.

Dr. Cutler also mentions the elegant wife of Elbridge Gerry, recently married, and comments on the sprightliness of the women in Philadelphia at half-past five breakfasts, when they could barely get down at nine in Boston without having hysterics. With such an agreeable meeting place and many hospitable homes about Philadelphia, it could not be expected that gentlemen of the Convention would confine their thoughts entirely to Convention matters. There were afternoon teas and dinner parties all over town and some of the delegates no doubt, from time to time, participated in the convivialities proffered by these occasions.

In Dr. Cutler's famous journal, mention is made of a trip to Bartram's Botanical Gardens with breakfast at Gray's Tavern on the south side of the Schuylkill river, on Saturday July 14, 1787. Dr. Cutler reported that the company included Dr. Hugh Williamson and Governor Martin of North Carolina, Caleb Strong, George Mason, author of the Bill of Rights, James Madison, "Father of the Constitution," and Alexander Hamilton. They were met by William Bartram, the world renowned botanist. Mr. Bartram was hoeing in his garden while wearing a short coat and trousers, and was bare-footed. He was the author of *Travels in the Carolinas*, a search for botanical specimens.[17] Dr. Cutler and Dr. Williamson must have been particularly congenial, as their lives met at many points. Both of them are remembered as ministers of the Gospel, doctors of medicine, soldiers, and members of the Congress of the United States. Dr. Cutler was then a member of the Continental Congress and one of the supposed authors of the Northwest Ordinance. This distinguished visitor in Philadelphia was also a sailor and whaler, a lawyer and a judge, a botanist, and an explorer in other fields. He and Dr. Williamson were members of numerous scientific societies and both won reputations as astronomers, Dr. Cutler in his studies on the Transit of Mercury over the Sun and the Eclipse of the Moon and Dr. Williamson on like perambulations of Venus and Mercury, with added dissertations on the migration of Comets.

They were also land speculators, one operating to the north of the Ohio River and the other to the south. Dr. Williamson was interested in some of William Blount's operations and prepared maps of the western country. No doubt Blount would have enjoyed the festivities of this gathering had he not been absent, attending the Continental Congress in New York. What dreams of speculation and empire building this breakfast company must have had! With two astronomers like Dr. Cutler and Dr. Williamson guiding the first feast of the day, the sky must have been the limit of their visions and aspirations.

It is not known what effect Dr. Cutler's high powered salesman-
ship had on our North Carolina deputies, some of whom were by
no means novices in the business. It has been said that about fifty
percent of the deputies including General Washington were speculators in government lands, or securities. Dr. Cutler was evidently
laying the foundations for a "land office business," such as was
already in progress in the Southwest territory, with such delegate-
participants as William Blount, Dr. Williamson, and other members of the Governor Caswell party. Many of these, no doubt, had
cut their teeth on the training which Judge Richard Henderson and
his Transylvanians had given them a decade before in the Kentucky Country. A fine picture could be drawn of this distinguished
gathering and the guests of the Indian Queen with a sprinkling of
imagination and a little spare time. This was shortly before
pioneer Cutler began his trek westward with his caravan marked
"Ohio, for Marietta on the Muskingum."

Dr. Williamson's varied career of scholar, educator, student of
divinity, doctor of medicine, merchant, soldier, patriot, statesman, scientist, author, and traveller, shows his versatility, and his
North Carolina associates recognized his worth. Correspondence
of the period, indicating the votes of thanks to him by the
Assembly, and the many trusts reposed in him, abundantly
disclose his value. He was certainly one of the most learned
members of the Federal Convention. Thomas Jefferson, who sat
with him in the Continental Congress at Annapolis, said that he
was a "very useful member of the Congress of the Confederation,
of acute mind and of a high degree of erudition"; and his
colleague, Pierce, in the Constitutional Convention, referred to
him as a gentleman of "education and talents with a great deal of
humor and pleasantry in his character."[18] Opposing views were
expressed by others like the able but acid-tongued Scot, Archibald Maclaine, and also a French observer reported by Farrand,
both of whom may have encountered the ill will of the doctor for

he was sometimes abrupt and even rude towards those who did not command his respect.[19]

Dr. Williamson's pen was active for ratifying the Constitution which the Convention signed on September 17, 1787. He published a paper in the *State Gazette of North Carolina* as follows:[20]

> It seems to be generally admitted, that the system of government which has been proposed by the late convention, is well calculated to relieve us from many of the grievances under which we have been laboring. If I might express my particular sentiments on this subject, I should describe it as more free and more perfect than any form of government that has ever been adopted by any nation; but I would not say it has no faults. Imperfection is inseparable from every device. Several objections were made to this system by two or three very respectable characters in the convention, which have been the subject of much conversation;

> "When you refer the proposed system to the particular circumstances of North Carolina, and consider how she is to be affected by this plan, you must find the utmost reason to rejoice in the prospect of better times. This is a sentiment that I have ventured with the greater confidence, because it is the general opinion of my late honorable colleagues, and I have the utmost reliance in their superior abilities. But if our constituents shall discover faults where we could not see any—or if they shall suppose that a plan is formed for abridging their liberties, when we imagined that we had been securing both liberty and property on a more stable foundation—if they perceive that they are to suffer a loss, where we thought they must rise from a misfortune,—they will, at least do us the justice to charge those errors to the head, and not to the heart."

When the Hillsboro Convention on July 21, 1788, nearly a year after the Constitution was signed, took the position neither to ratify nor reject but to make delay, until the Bill of Rights should be incorporated in it, Dr. Williamson, then in the Continental Congress, said that want of honesty was back of the opposition. He wrote an apology for North Carolina which appeared in the *New York Daily Advertiser*, on September 17, 1788, and immediately thereafter in the *State Gazette of North Carolina*, at Edenton. He took pains to call attention to the resolution of the Hillsboro Convention about collecting imposts and turning them over to the general government and concluded that North Carolina in time would support the federal government.[21]

The opposition in North Carolina was intense. The anti-Federalists seemed to fear that too much power had been delegated to the general government; that the commerce clause would enable the states to her north and to her south to throttle her commerce; that the treaty-making powers of the Senate would cripple her control of her western lands and interfere with her Mississippi outlet to the sea; and, particularly, that personal security and personal liberty had not been protected sufficiently when the Bill of Rights met failure of incorporation in the Constitution.

There was also a great deal of opposition among the fighting Scotch-Irish. Old General Matthew Locke, with four sons and a numerous clan of kinsmen, all veterans of the war and all rich in land and slaves, was one of the pioneers for manhood suffrage. He stated in the ratifying Convention that the whole arrangement was too expensive and that North Carolina could get along better alone than in the combination.[22] He and other intense Republicans who had been on the firing line since the inception of the troubles with England, adhered strongly to the principles of local self government as contained in the free, sovereign, and independent State of North Carolina. Most of the opponents of the Constitution wanted a Bill of Rights placed in the Constitution *before* and not *after* ratification. This sentiment was one of the main blocks to ratification in such states as North Carolina, Massachusetts, New York, Pennsylvania, and Virginia. A new Convention had been suggested to revamp the Constitution as submitted, for the purpose of overcoming the above and other objections raised in these rebellious states. Anticipations of a new Convention were very much alive in North Carolina. The General Assembly, meeting in Fayetteville contemporaneously with the ratifying Convention, actually chose old rebels like Gen. Thomas Person, Timothy Bloodworth, Gen. Matthew Locke, Col. Joseph McDowell, and Gen. William Lenoir as delegates to such a new Convention, which the New York and Virginia assemblies had already asked the Congress to call.[23] But the first Congress under the Constitution, meeting March 4, 1789, out of the vast number proposed by the several states submitted twelve amendments. Ten of these were soon adopted by the requisite number of states. On December 22, 1789, North Carolina was one of four States to vote approval of all twelve amendments. On November 21, 1789, feeling assured that she would have her cherished Bill of Rights, or be left out of the new organization. North Carolina ratified the Constitution and became a member of the Union, under the Constitution.

Due credit has never been given to Dr. Hugh Williamson for his intense interest in the ratification of the Federal Constitution. None of our local historians, so far as has been observed, has ever credited him with moving the resolution of adoption. After an appropriate preamble which among other things set forth the language of the Constitution, and which on his motion, seconded by Mr. Blount, had been read before the Convention, he resolved as follows:

> Resolved, That this Convention, in behalf of the freeman, citizens, and inhabitants of the State of North Carolina, do adopt and ratify the said Constitution and form of government.

This motion was referred to a Committee of the whole house and several days were consumed before the Committee reported. On the 20th, the Committee reported a resolution concurring with the Williamson preamble and resolution. It was ordered that the resolution be tabled until the 21st. On that day, after several amendments were proposed and rejected, Mr. Davie moved that the Convention concur with this Committee resolution, which was in the same language as the original Williamson preamble and resolution. On the yeas and nays being called, the motion carried in the affirmative by a vote of 195 to 77.[24] So the Constitution of the United States, in reality, was adopted on the resolution of Williamson, though the final motion on his resolution as concurred in by the Committee of the whole house, was made by Davie.

Many things had transpired in North Carolina's relationship to the old and the new government since the new Constitution had been sent to the Congress of the Confederation and, on September 28, submitted by it to the states for their consideration. Only two more sessions of the old Congress were held, one from November 5, 1787 to October 21, 1788, and the other from November 3, 1788 to March 2, 1789. North Carolina elected delegates to both of these sessions, but the records only show attendance upon the first by Dr. Hugh Williamson, Robert Burton, and Dr. James White, and upon the second by Dr. Hugh Williamson, Dr. James White, and John Swann, who took the place of John Baptista Ashe.[25]

It is of interest that Dr. James White was the grandfather of Chief Justice Edward Douglas White. He was a native of Pennsylvania and was educated in France. After settling a while in Salisbury he moved west to the Nashville neighborhood of the state. Everything was in a state of change. The old government was suffering the sting of death; the new, the pangs of birth. On April 21, 1788, Dr. James White wrote the governor that he was on the eve of leaving the Congress as scarcely a competent number of states had assembled during the whole winter and that even the New York delegation had neglected its attendance. He reported the news from Dr. Williamson that he and John Swann would attend the Congress. As the Articles of Confederation provided that no state should be represented by less than two members, North Carolina could not vote.[26] Dr. Williamson wrote the governor, from New York on May 30, 1788, that Swann had arrived, giving the State the first vote since October, 1787.[27] Dr. Williamson attended until November 3, and as late as March 9, 1789 he wrote that he had not been absent a single day.[28]

When New Hampshire, the ninth State, ratified the Constitution on June 21, 1788, the work of the Constitutional Convention was approved by the requisite number. But many people doubted the ability of the new government to function, in the absence of such important states as Virginia, North Carolina, and New York. Dr. Williamson wrote on July 29, 1788, that New York had ratified the Constitution and that the Congress was extremely desirous of fixing a time and place to begin proceedings, but that the first session had been delayed in part out of deference to the feelings of North Carolina.[29] He was very anxious for North Carolina to come into the union and cited France's complaint of state protection to one of her pirates as the "mournful need" of an organized government.

James Madison expressed the situation clearly when he said that the non-ratifying states must either come in or be left as outcasts from the new society. When North Carolina declined unconditional ratification on August 4, 1788, she made a gesture of interest by resolving to collect imposts and to turn them over to the United States; but she was left outside in the none-too-congenial company of Rhode Island; Virginia, the eleventh State, ratified on June 25, 1788. Samuel Johnston, the president of the Hillsboro Convention, warned it to pause a moment before deciding so important a question, saying that North Carolina could neither propose an amendment nor vote on one after it had been submitted. "In my humble opinion," he said, "we shall be entirely out of the Union and can be considered only as a foreign power."[30]

The old Congress, on September 13, 1788, passed a resolution to put the new Constitution in operation and fixed the first Wednesday in January for choosing presidential electors, the first Wednesday in February for their meeting, and the first Wednesday in March for the first session of the Congress, to be held in New York. In none of these movements could North Carolina participate. It is doubtful if North Carolina is entitled to all the credit some claim for forcing adoption of the Bill of Rights, or for passage of the first ten amendments. There was bitter hostility to the Constitution in Virginia, Pennsylvania, Massachusetts, and New York over their omission. They also resented the failure to call a second convention to consider all wanted amendments, before the final vote on ratification. These States entered the union when they considered they could best influence amendments, among others the Bill of Rights that some of them suggested when they ratified the Constitution. North Carolina stayed out, so that it had no influence. North Carolina came in, finally, after the Congress of September 25, 1789, submitted the amendments so much desired and ten of which were so speedily ratified by the needed nine states in the Union. Their omission in the original Constitution was quite generally admitted to have been a mistake.

Governor Samuel Johnston wrote to Dr. Hugh Williamson on September 22, 1788, that it certainly was necessary for North Carolina to be represented in the federal councils. In the mountain areas, North Carolina, South Carolina, and Georgia were troubled with Indian massacres. Under the Articles of Confederation, the Congress was given authority over Indian affairs where its action did not encroach upon the states. Many wanted Congress to have complete control over Indian affairs.

The Hopewell Treaty with the Indians was causing embarrassment to the Governor and to Dr. Williamson, as it gave land to the

Indians which had previously been ceded to the State. These lands had been settled by some 1500 white people south of the French Broad and Holston rivers. The safety of the women and children was imperiled. In September the new Congress appropriated money and sent a commission to Georgia to make a treaty with the southern Indians. National conditions were becoming more precarious at every turn and Williamson's position was weakening. Sensing the probability that Williamson would no longer have a seat after receipt of his letter, Governor Johnston said to him, on February 19, 1789: "I shall notwithstanding hope that you will still consider yourself a *Confidential Servant* of the State and that you will occasionally communicate to me every matter of a public nature in which you may consider this State to be interested which may come to your knowledge."[31]

On March 9, 1789, the *Confidential Servant* wrote that sundry members, according to appointment, namely 8 senators and 14 of the House of Representatives, met at the public building in New York. Since that time, he said, the members of the old Congress had not attempted to form a house, as most of those who were not in the new Congress had gone home. A quorum of the New Congress did not assemble until the 6th of April. Dr. Williamson was manfully hanging on. He graphically showed his tenacity when he wrote on the 23rd of March, that he was still claiming the right of franking his letters, but he said the new government doubtless would dispute this privilege.[32]

The situation was reaching a crisis. There was no longer any doubt about North Carolina being out of the Union. There was some debate about it, after the nine states had ratified; but now she clearly was not in the new arrangement which began functioning with solidarity when George Washington on April 30, 1789, took the oath of office as President of the United States of America.

The *Confidential Servant*, with no credentials except the governor's letter, soon felt the responsibility of being the sole repre-

sentative of the free, sovereign, and independent State of North
Carolina. The Congress fixed the relationship. On July 31, 1789, it
abolished collecting duties within the limits of Rhode Island and
North Carolina, but enacted a law that goods imported from these
two states into any port or place within the limits of the United
States should be "subject to like duties, seizures, and forfeitures,
as goods etc., imported from any state or country without the said
limits."[33] This made the separation a reality. Dr. Williamson had
called the governor's attention to the new revenue system, on
April 30, and said that it would place a heavy burden on the
commerce of North Carolina, and throw many persons engaged in
commerce out of employment. He complained of the one dollar
duty per hogshead on various articles, saying that previous
indications concerned only a duty on naval stores and corn. He
also said that the foreign tonnage duty of half-dollar per ton must
nip North Carolina's trade. Calculating five hundred vessels
annually clearing from the state at 40 tons each, the tax would be
about $10,000, thus causing a reduction in the value of the state's
produce since it had no monopoly. He further regretted being out
of the Union, as members in the Union would be of great aid to the
state in promoting ship building. With some success he besought
Congress to suspend duties on home-owned vessels until January
15, 1790, presumably to give his state a little more time to enter
the Union. He expressed fear that his wishes might be thwarted
by the numerous petitions coming in from Rhode Island. "These
people seem to be asking things that are not safely to be granted,"
said he, as he mildly expressed his dislike of this company outside
the Union.[34]

Other acts of sovereignty were performed for the state by its
Confidential Servant. He prepared a memorial requesting the
Minister of France to relieve the state of the embarrassing
requirement of clearing all vessels for the French West Indies
through Wilmington, when three-fourths of the trade normally
cleared through Ocracoke.[35] There were many things transpiring

like the troubles with Spain, growing out of the Mississippi outlet, and the disputes with the Indians. There were further complications when North Carolina was not included in the federal judiciary act of 1789. Judge James Iredell had been proposed for one of the justices of the Supreme Court. He wrote Dr. Williamson that he might be disposed to leave the state to fill such an appointment, if it were necessary to do so.[36] Dr. Williamson also helped with the French correspondence about North Carolina's debt to France.

The General Assembly in 1788 had appointed Hugh Williamson, then a member of the Continential Congress, and Abishai Thomas as agents to settle the army accounts between North Carolina and the Confederation, which also had a Board of Commissioners working on this intricate matter. Dr. Williamson was a member of the Board of Treasury of the United States and also a member of the above commission. He accepted the State appointment and received the thanks of the governor, who expressed the high confidence entertained by the state in his abilities. In reply Dr. Williamson remarked that settling old and intricate accounts was not the best commission he had ever held.[37] When the General Assembly of 1789 chartered the University with his name among the first of the original Trustees, the Assembly really touched his heart with the kind of honor he preferred.

His convention colleague Col. William R. Davie, was chairman of the finance committee in the General Assembly and reported that there were no musters of two whole battalions, nor of many individuals who had served in the Revolution. It was necessary to gather together such fragmentary evidences as were left of the services of our state and her soldiers in the Revolution by examining the accounts and proceedings of the governor and his council, letters and orders of the generals and officers of the Continental line, the journals of the provincial and state congresses, and the minutes of the committees of safety in the various counties, and their records as to equipment, supplies, and pay for soldiers in the Continental line, and in the militia. It was also necessary to get into contact with officers and privates still living, and with the executors, administrators, widows, and children of those who had died, so that muster rolls could be completed. Extensive search was made for all vouchers showing such expenses as North Carolina had incurred in the fight for liberty and independence. Mr. Thomas was in North Carolina most of the time, working with the comptroller of the state and others, and Dr. Williamson was in New York in constant service on the Board of Commissioners of the Continential Congress, endeavoring to ascertain how other states were handling their accounts and suggesting what was necessary in order to best present the account of North Carolina. It readily may be seen how much simpler it was to dump the whole business on the general government as it soon was done. The state is indebted, however, to its agents for making what records it has of the services performed by North Carolina soldiers, who were rushed into action in large numbers without any regard for preserving their patriotic achievements.

These services of Dr. Williamson were continued after he ceased to be a member of the expiring Congress of the Confederation and became a member of the Congress of the United States of America, to which office he was elected from the Edenton district. He took his seat as the first representative to qualify from North Carolina on March 19, 1790. North Carolina did not join the union in time to send members to the first session of the first Congress but her five members qualified for the second session.

This Congress inherited the task of adjusting the debts and claims of the several states, and Dr. Williamson served on a committee to prepare a bill for making speedy settlement of these public accounts.[38] He wrote home that he hoped North Carolina would be a creditor state and outlined the various plans suggested for making the final settlement. The whole business of settling the accounts was finally referred to a select committee of which Dr.

Williamson was made a member. At this time the question of the assumption of the state debts by the general government was receiving considerable attention. Dr. Williamson seemed, from a letter written on March 20, to have opposed the assumption of state debts. He said such an act would add too greatly to national taxes and that North Carolina would not only be deprived of getting credit for what she already had spent but would be taxed to pay the debts of the bankrupt states. He stated that New England and New York, together with parts of New Jersey and Pennsylvania and South Carolina strongly favored assumption. Alexander Hamilton had made his financial report as Secretary of the Treasury and assumption was one of his recommendations. The North Carolina delegation, which had just entered Congress, turned the tide against assumption and defeated it when the bill first came before the House.[39] Hamilton then saw the necessity for getting a Southern leader on his side. He made the famous bargain with Secretary of State Jefferson, the latter to deliver the necessary votes, in return for which the seat of government would be placed on the Potomac.[40] The bill fixing the seat of Government passed on July 16, and the consolidated funding and assumption bill on August 4, 1790. Dr. Williamson fell in line with Hamilton's "American Policy" when the excise tax for raising revenue was presented, though it was very unpopular in his district.[41] He had no love for whiskey in any of its aspects and wrote at length about its bad effects. In the second Congress he also sat as a member, but did not stand for a seat in the third Congress. In the third Congress his census suggestion was beginning to bear fruit, for North Carolina doubled her representation after the census of 1790 had disclosed her standing in the third place among the original thirteen states.

In January, 1789, he married Maria Apthorpe, daughter of Honorable Charles Ward Apthorpe, formerly a member of His Majesty's Council for New York.[42] After voluntarily deciding to leave Congress, he made his home in New York. His wife died soon after the birth of their second son. His oldest son, who was very promising and was just reaching manhood, died in 1811 and the youngest son died soon thereafter. Amid all of these afflications, Dr. Williamson's grief was partially assuaged by the congenial pursuit of literature and philosophy. In 1811 appeared his *Observations on the Climate in Different Parts of America, Compared with the Climate in Corresponding Parts of the Other Continents*. This was the first American work on this subject and was largely in answer to the aspersions of writers who had reflected upon the climate of North America. It was intended as an introduction to his *History of North Carolina*, which was published in 1812.

In the introduction to his *History of North Carolina* he says that he had contemplated covering a fuller period of North Carolina history. The death of his promising son may have discouraged further effort on his part, for he sent the manuscript to the printers soon after his son's death. It covers a dull period of slow growth, civil strife, maladministrations of unprincipled executives and intensely disorganized individualism in the life of North Carolina. He did very well with the scant material he had, and told a clear, simple, readable story. Dr. Williamson was much more scientific than literary in his talents and he was inclined to be crisp and brief in keeping with his mathematically inclined mind. His history seems not to have met the expectations of some of his critics while, on the other hand, it also has been classed with Stith and other leading historians of the Colonial periods of our States. That he did not cover the revolutionary and pre-revolutionary period with which he was so familiar poses a great loss to the State. He could have told "how difficult a part had fallen to the share of our State in the course of the business" before the Constitutional Convention. He had written the Governor at the close of the Convention that he hoped some day to be able to do.[43]

He was very active in helping to arrange some of the most important compromises out of which the Constitution grew, for he served on many of the leading committees, where his talents best displayed themselves, as he did not have the shining gifts of a speaker to make much of a floor display. A resume shows he was in favor of settling the dispute over representation in the legislative branch, by making it equal in the Senate and proportional in the House; he was in favor of extending the bounds of slavery importation, though very much opposed to the system, because he thought it better to risk the concession than to lose the Constitution; and, for the same reason, suggested he was in favor of counting five slaves as three, to appease the South. He also had a give and take attitude on assumption of war debts, location of the seat of government, placing commerce under control of the general government, and ceding the western lands, always trading as best he could for the interest of his adopted state. His long legislative experience had taught him that compromise was sometimes necessary to effect legislation.

He wrote many short papers for various publications in the field of Natural History, Medicine, and Philosophy, among them: on fevers of North Carolina, as they prevailed in 1792, on the Roanoke River; on the fascination of serpents; on the incorrect manner in which iron rods are sometimes set up for defending houses from lightning; on navigable canals; on means of Preserving the Commerce of New York; on the benefits of civil history; *What is Sauce for the Goose is also Sauce for a Gander, An Epitaph on a Certain Great Man* (1764); *Observation on the Proposed State Road from Hudson's River . . . to Lake Erie* (1800); and many others. He was one of the first men in New York to propose the building of a canal from Lake Erie to the Hudson River. A series of articles were published by him under the name of Atticus. These articles had wide circulation in the papers of the day and were published many times in pamphlet form.

In 1805 Dr. Williamson was appointed by the corporation of the City of New York on a medical committee to investigate the origin of yellow fever, which was one of the pestilences of that day. He was also associated with Governor DeWitt Clinton and other gentlemen in the formation of the Literary and Philosophical Society of New York, contributing a valuable paper to the first volume of its transactions. He was a Trustee of the College of Physicians and Surgeons of the University of the State of New York, to which he liberally contributed both his time and his money. The Orphan Asylum, the Society for the Relief of the Poor Widows with Small Children, the Humane Society, and the City Dispensary of the New York Hospital were beneficiaries of his generous enthusiasm and help. His versatility enabled him to occupy his time with both profit and pleasure to himself and to his community. [45]

Washington Irving, in his life of George Washington, tells an interesting story of the meeting between "the honest doctor" and Cerrachi, the celebrated Italian sculptor, republican idealist, and plotter against the life of Napoleon. [46] Cerrachi conceived a "Grand National Monument Commemorative of American Independence," to be erected in Washington. In furtherance of his design he made a signal success of a bust of Washington, "generally considered the most perfect combined representation of the man and the hero, after Stuart's and Houdon's masterpieces." Cerrachi likewise had made busts of Hamilton, Jay, Trumbull, and Clinton. He then sought the unwilling offices of Dr. Williamson, whom he also expressed a wish to portray. Washington Irving gives this account of what transpired between them:

> The zeal of Cerrachi in his cherished purpose, is indicated by the assurance he gave Dr. Hugh Williamson—the historian of North Carolina, and the author of the earliest work on the American Climate, and one of the first advocates of the canal policy—when inviting him to sit for his bust, that he did not pay him the compliment in order to secure his vote for the national monument, but only to perpetuate the 'features of the American Cato.'

With characteristic emphasis, the honest doctor declined, on the ground that posterity would not care for his lineaments; adding that, 'if he were capable of being lured into the support of any scheme whatever, against his conviction of right, wood, and not stone, ought to be the material of his image.'

On May 22, 1819, while out riding in New York with Maria Vanden Heuvel Hamilton, his wife's niece and the wife of John C. Hamilton, son of Alexander Hamilton, Dr. Williamson, as he had predicted, died suddenly. He was in his eighty-fifth year. He was tenderly attached to his favorite niece and in his will stated that, at his request, she "was named Maria, the name of my beloved wife." He left her, among other property, his home at 229 Broadway "in which she now (1818) resides" and where his funeral was held. Dr. Hugh Williamson was buried in Trinity Church Graveyard, near the remains of Alexander Hamilton with whom he had collaborated in helping to frame our Federal Constitution.

LIST OF THE MEMBERS
OF THE FEDERAL CONVENTION WHICH FORMED
THE CONSTITUTION OF THE UNITED STATES

(Senate Document Number 728–Sixtieth Congress, Second Session)

From		Attended
New Hampshire...	1. John Langdon..................	July 23, 1787
	John Pickering,	
	2. Nicholas Gilman	July 23, 1787
	Benjamin West.	
Massachusetts	*Francis Dana,*	
	Elbridge Gerry................	May 29, 1787
	3. Nathaniel Gorham.............	May 28, 1787
	4. Rufus King	May 25, 1787
	Caleb Strong..................	May 28, 1787
Rhode Island	(No appointment.)	
Connecticut	5. Wm. Sam Johnson	June 2, 1787
	6. Roger Sherman	May 30, 1787
	Oliver Ellsworth	May 29, 1787
New York........	Robert Yates	May 25, 1787
	7. Alexander Hamilton	May 25, 1787
	John Lansing	June 2, 1787
New Jersey.......	8. Wm. Livingston..............	June 5, 1787
	9. David Brearley................	May 25, 1787
	William C. Houston	May 25, 1787
	10. William Paterson	May 25, 1787
	John Nielson,	
	Abraham Clark,	
	11. Jonathan Dayton	June 21, 1787
Pennsylvania	12. Benjamin Franklin.............	May 28, 1787
	13. Thomas Mifflin...............	May 28, 1787
	14. Robert Morris................	May 25, 1787
	15. George Clymer...............	May 28, 1787
	16. Thos. Fitzsimons.............	May 25, 1787
	17. Jared Ingersoll	May 28, 1787
	18. James Wilson	May 25, 1787
	19. Gouverneur Morris	May 25, 1787
Delaware.........	20. George Read..................	May 25, 1787
	21. Gunning Bedford, Jr.	May 28, 1787
	22. John Dickinson	May 23, 1787

From		Attended
State	Name	Date
	23. Richard Bassett	May 25, 1787
	24. Jacob Broom	May 25, 1787
Maryland.........	25. James M'Henry	May 29, 1787
	26. Daniel of St. Thomas Jenifer....	June 2, 1787
	27. Daniel Carroll................	July 9, 1787
	John Francis Mercer..........	August 6, 1787
	Luther Martin.................	June 9, 1787
Virginia	28. George Washington...........	May 25, 1787
	Patrick Henry................	(Declined.)
	29. John Blair	May 25, 1787
	30. James Madison, Jr............	May 25, 1787
	George Mason	May 25, 1787
	George Wythe	May 25, 1787
	James M'Clurg, (in the room of P. Henry.)	May 25, 1787
North Carolina....	*Richard Caswell*..............	(Resigned.)
	Alexander Martin	May 25, 1787
	William R. Davie.............	May 25, 1787
	31. William Blount, (in the room of R. Caswell.)	June 20, 1787
	Willie Jones	(Declined.)
	32. Richard D. Spaight	May 25, 1787
	33. Hugh Williamson, (in the room of W. Jones.)	May 25, 1787
South Carolina....	34. John Rutledge................	May 25, 1787
	35. Charles C. Pinkney	May 25, 1787
	36. Charles Pinckney.............	May 25, 1787
	37. Pierce Butler.................	May 25, 1787
Georgia	38. William Few	May 25, 1787
	39. Abraham Baldwin	June 11, 1787
	William Pierce	May 31, 1787
	George Walton,	
	William Houston	June 1, 1787
	Nathaniel Pendleton.	

Those with numbers before their names, signed the constitution 39
Those in italics, never attended 10
Members who attended, but did not sign the constitution 16
                                                                       65

FOOTNOTES TO FOREWORD

1. Ecclesiastes, 1:9.
2. Familiar letters of John Adams and his wife, Abigail Adams, during the Revolution. p. 205.
3. Hannis Taylor, A Memorial in Behalf of the Architec of Our Constitution, Peletiah Webster (a contemporary) of Philadelphia, p. 50, being Senate Document 461, 6th Congress. First Session.
4. Max Farrand, *The Records of the Federal Convention,* III, 530. (Hereafter cited, as Farrand). Edmund Cody Burnett, The Continental Congress, 480. North Carolina was the first State to suggest impost duties. (Source Quotation) Proceedings & Debates of Convention of North Carolina, at Hillsboro in 1788, 40.
5. The State Records of North Carolina, XVIII, 681, 2, 3. (Hereafter cited as N.C.S.R.)
6. N.C.S.R., XVIII, 683, 659, 660, 661.
7. N.C.S.R., XVIII, 692.
8. N.C.S.R., XVIII, 773, 683.
9. Same.
10. Same.
11. Gaillard Hunt and James B. Scott, *Debates in the Federal Convention of 1787,* reported by James Madison, L, LIII. (Hereafter quoted as Hunt & Scott).
12. Hunt & Scott, LIV, LV. Edmund Cody Burnett, *The Continental Congress,* (1941), Chap. XXXIV. Good account, also of the closing days of the Continental Congress.

FOOTNOTES TO CHAPTER I

1. Hunt & Scott, LIII, LXXIV. N.C.S.R., XXIV, 791. Edmund Cody Burnett, *The Continental Congress,* 667 et seq., 678. For general discussion, see *The Federalist* No. XL by Madison.
2. N.C.S.R., XVIII, 462.
3. N.C.S.R., XX, 129.
4. Original Constitution in Library of Congress. Farrand, II, 664.
5. Charles Warren, *The Making of the Constitution,* 55. James Franklin Jameson, IV. *Studies in the History of the Federal Convention* of 1787, 157. See list at end hereof.
6. Hunt & Scott, LXXXIII et seq. Herein also at LVI et seq. are copies of the credentials of the members of the Convention. Farrand III, 135. Jameson, 157; also, chart at end of these papers.
7. Farrand, LXVII.
8. Princeton Alumni Weekly, Vol. XXIX, No. 34, Article by Prof. Walter Lincoln Whittlesey. Letter from A. Guyot Cameron of Princeton. Cornelia Rebecca Shaw, Davidson College, 2.
8. Charles A. Beard, *An Economic Interpretation of the Constitution,* 287.
9. World Almanac, 1942, 587 (census, population) Marshall DeLancey Haywood, *Governor Tryon of North Carolina,* 59-60. Same, *N.C. Booklet,* 15, 32, (on troops).
10. N.C.S.R. XX, 778. Letter from Blount, Spaight, and Williamson, Sept. 18, 1787, to Governor Caswell.
11. Vol. 29, Reports North Carolina Bar Association 1927, 27, Speech of Honorable Claude G. Bowers.
12. For a discussion of North Carolina Annapolis delegates see foreword and Sketch of Dr. Hugh Williamson.
13. Gilbert Chinard, *Honest John Adams,* 99. Familiar Letter of John Adams and His Wife, Number 123, 204.
14. James Madison's *Notes* and a *Society of Nations* 34, by James Brown Scott, quoting *Documentary History of the Constitution,* III, 160. One of the first notes from the Convention of this predicted dispute occurs in a letter dated New York, July 19, from William Blount to John Gray Blount (Burnett, Letters of Members of the Continental Congress, VIII, 623). This was after the dispute was settled; it must have been information gathered by Blount before July 3, when he said he arrived in New York from Philadelphia. Blount said: "The little States were much opposed to the Politics of the larger. They insisted that each State ought to have an equal vote as in the present confederation." He was overstepping the Convention rules of secrecy. He further said that our delegation was in sentiment with Virginia which seemed to take the lead. He evidently had not heard of the vote of North Carolina and her switch from Virginia domination.

14a. *Basic History of the United States,* Charles and Mary Beard, 135.

15. *A Memorial in Behalf of the Architect of Our Constitution,* Peletiah Webster of Philadelphia, with a Dissertation on the Political Union and Constitution of the Thirteen United States of America by him, with his notes, Hannis Taylor, 50, being Senate Document No. 461, 6th Congress, first session. Dr. Taylor held an LL.D. from the Universities of North Carolina, Alabama, Mississippi, Tulane, Washington & Lee, Dublin, and Edinburgh and was a native of New Bern, N.C. See Chapter VI, Hannis Taylor's *Origin and Growth of the Constitution. Great Debates in American History,* Vol. 1, 272. The First Constitution of North Carolina expressly provided that the Legislative, Executive, and Judicial departments are to be forever separate and distinct from one another. This idea, first enunciated among English people by John Locke, (Of Civil Government, 2nd Treatise, Chap. IX, Page 124) is said to have been suggested for our Constitution by John Adams with whom Governor Burke, or Governor Caswell, consulted before framing it. Governor Swain said Burke; Captain Ashe thought Caswell. Ashe, Vol. I, 561. Hannis Taylor, *The Origin and Growth of the English Constitution,* 1, 58, et seq.

16. *The Diplomatic Correspondence of the American Revolution,* edited under direction of Congress by Francis Wharton, Vol. 6, 97. Francis Newton Thorpe, *The Constitutional History of the United States,* 1, 307, N.I.

17. Farrand, III, 56. This was when Yates and Lansing left the Convention.

18. *The Making of the Constitution,* 155. Charles Warren. (Hereafter Warren). Farrand I and II (1937).

19. Farrand I and II (1937).

20. Joseph Reese Strayer, *The Delegate from New York* (1939). Secret Proceedings & Debates, etc., Senate Document No. 728 Sixtieth Congress, Second Session, 1909.

21. As Madison's *Notes* were kept from day to day and so arranged and dated, . . . they may be followed easily. See, also, Ferrand, or Alliot's *Debates,* or Galliard Hunt and James Scott, or Charles Warren, or Charles C. Tansill (Langing's Notes), or *Secret Proceedings and Debates* (Yates's Minutes), or *Documentary History of the Constitution,* or others referred to in this work. Ferrand is the most complete and the latest compilation. Farrand, I, 29, 33, 38, May 30, showing reference to the Committee of the whole House.

22. Hunt and Scott, 27. Farrand, I, 176, 181, 184, June 9.

23. Hunt and Scott, 80.

24. Farrand, 1, 177-179. Hunt and Scott, 81-83.

25. Farrand, 1, 179. Hunt and Scott, 83.

26. Farrand, 1, 196. Hunt and Scott, 84, June 11, Connecticut had somewhat similar organization. Woodrow Wilson, *The State,* 473. Breckenridge Long, *Genesis of the Constitution,* 38, 40.
27. Hunt and Scott, 88, 89.
28. Farrand, 1, 202.
29. Farrand, 1, 202.
30. Farrand, 1, 240.
31. Farrand, 1, 253.
32. Farrand, 1, 322.
33. Farrand, 1, 407.
34. Farrand, 1, 450-452.
35. Farrand, 1, 452.
36. Farrand, 1, 445.
37. Farrand, 1, 458, Yates's Minutes. For the Divine Inspiration that guided the Convention see von Holst, *Constitutional History of the United States,* 1, 63 note.
38. Farrand, 1, 468.
39. Farrand, 1, 468.
40. Farrand, 1, 487-8. 498 (Yates's Minutes). *The Delegates from New York* (Lansing) 98, by Joseph R. Strayer — See n. 156.
41. Professor Hubbard's *Life of William Richardson Davie* in The Library of American Biography by Sparks, Vol. XV, New Series, 132.
42. Farrand, 1, 488.
43. Farrand, 1, 481-490.
44. Farrand, 1, 177, 178, Warren, 199, 200. *Great Debates in American History,* 1, 270.
45. Farrand, 1, 490. *Democracy in America,* deTocqueville, 136. *Great Debates in American History* I, 270.
46. Farrand, 1, 490-2–500 (Yates's Minutes).
47. Warren, *The Making of the Constitution,* 272-277. (Hereafter Warren).
48. Farrand, 1, 510.
49. Warren, 262, n. 1.
50. Farrand, 511; Warren, 263.
51. Farrand, 1, 515.
52. Farrand, 1, 511.
53. Warren, 264, 272.
54. Farrand, 1, 516.
55. Farrand, 1, 524.
56. McRee's Life of Iredell, II, 162.
57. Farrand, 1, 526; Warren, 272. In the Convention discussions, there were three propositions, as enumerated above, though I and II were consolidated in the Report of the Committee.

58. Farrand, 1, 526.
59. Farrand, 1, 527.
60. Farrand, 1, 527.
61. Farrand, 1, 527-8-9; but see Number LXII in *The Federalist*, by Madison.
62. Farrand, 1, 529-30-31.
63. Farrand, 1, 531.
63. Farrand, 1, 531.
64. Farrand, 1, 532.
65. Farrand, 1, 532.
66. Farrand, 1, 524. This was subsequently reduced to 30,000 by President Washington's only speech, Warren, 712.
67. Farrand, 1, 229, 7th Resolve.
68. Farrand, 1, 540.
69. Farrand, 1, 542.
70. Farrand, 1, 542.
71. Farrand, 1, 543.
72. Farrand, 1, 543.
73. Farrand, 1, 524.
74. Farrand, 1, 234, Warren, 275 and generally, 274-277.
75. Farrand, 1, 544.
76. Farrand, II, 233. Dr. Williamson, in the debate on the report, told the small states that the State of North Carolina had agreed to an equality in the Senate, merely in consideration that money bills should be confined to the other House and that he was surprised to see the smaller States forsaking the condition on which they had received their equality. See how Williamson finally helped in settling this troublesome question on Sept. 8, Warren, 664-670.
77. The report of the Grand Committee was founded on a motion in the Committee made by Dr. Franklin. It was barely acquiesced in by the opposition and was thought by those favoring it, as gaining their point. Farrand, 1, 526. It was always important that people should know who had disposed of their money and that money affairs should be confined to the immediate representatives of the people. This was Dr. Franklin's inducement to concur in the Report. Farrand 1, 546. See also: Thorpe 1, 428; Thorpe III, 484, 485; Warren 275; Hendricks 85, Note 116; Hunt & Scott 206, note; and Farrand III, 265.
78. Farrand 1, 527, 529, Warren, 275.
79. Farrand 1, 547, Warren, 277, giving N.C. the credit.
80. Farrand 1, 550. Elliot, 1, 507. James Madison to Mr. Sparks, April 8, 1831, discussing the Crisis in the Convention, 44 years after the event.
81. Farrand 1, 551.
82. Farrand 1, 559.

83. Farrand 1, 559.
84. Farrand 1, 559.
85. Farrand 1, 560.
86. Farrand 1, 560-61, Curtis, 11, 153.
87. Farrand 1, 562.
88. Farrand 1, 563.
89. Farrand 1, 533, 534.
90. Elliot's Debates in the Congress of the Confederation, (Supplement to Elliot's Debates) V, 44. Geo. Leakin Sioussat, *The North Carolina Cession of 1784,* etc. 5. Having the same rule of apportionment for direct taxation and representation produced the requisite impartiality. *The Federalist* No. LIV.
91. Farrand, 1, 605.
92. Farrand, 1, 606.
93. Farrand, 1, 562.
94. Farrand, 1, 570.
95. Farrand, 1, 579.
96. Curtis, *History of the Constitution of the United States,* II, 160 et seq., also 1, 213, Notes 1 and 2, for discussion of 3/5 rule. Also generally II, Chapter VII, 145 et seq.
97. Farrand, 1, 579.
98. Farrand, 1, 580. Story, *Commentaries on the Constitution,* I, 112, says it was borrowed from a resolve of the Continental Congress, passed 4/18/1783.
99. Farrand, 5, 581.
100. *Biographical Directory of the American Congress,* 1774-1927, 35.
101. Bancroft, *History of the Constitution of the United States,* II, 81.
102. Farrand, I, 581, 588.
103. Farrand, I, 587.
104. Farrand, I, 588.
105. Farrand, I, 593, 229 (7), 579.
106. Farrand, I, 591-592.
107. Farrand, I, 592, 594, 595.
108. Farrand, I, 594, 595.
109. Farrand, I, 595, Curtis, Vol. II, 163.
110. Farrand, I, 597, 606. Hamilton and Madison in the *Federalist,* Number LV.
111. Farrand, II, 651.
112. Blount, Spaight, and Williamson to Governor Caswell, N.C.S.R. XX, 777.
113. Story, 2, 113.
114. 33 *Corpus Juris,* Internal Revenue, Sec. 40, 289, N.C. The first income

tax law was held unconstitutional, because it was a direct tax without apportionment.

115. Warren, 281, with lengthy discussion in notes. Bancroft, II, 74-75. Von Holst, 1, 51 and note, giving reasons. Great Debates, 1, 348, for lettter of Yates and Lansing to Governor Clinton.

116. Farrand, I, proceedings on July 16. Bancroft, II, 88. Burton J. Hendricks, *Bulwarks of the Constitution,* 86. Hannis Taylor, *The Origin and Growth of the American Constitution,* 199. Walter Clark, C.J. N.C.S.R., XX, VI.

117. Taylor, 199, 45, "From North Carolina came Alexander Martin, William R. Davie, Richard Dobbs Spaight and Hu Williamson, who at the critical moment prevented a catastrophe and saved the Convention from dissolution. When the Connecticut Compromise . . . was trembling in the balance, North Carolina saved the Convention by deserting her larger associates, thereby giving a majority to one of the Smaller States." When Thomas Jefferson in Paris heard of the success he wrote Madison on December 20, 1787: "I am captivated by the Compromise of the opposite claims of the great and little states, of the latter to equal and the former to proportional influence." *Jefferson's Complete Works* (1853), 2, 329.

118. Bancroft II, 88.

119, Hendricks, 86.

120. John Fiske, *The Critical Period of American History,* 252. Mr. Charles Warren, in *The Making of the Constitution,* 309, gives the same erroneous credit to his native state, Massachusetts.

121. Warren, 309, giving the Credit to Massachusetts.

122. Elliot's Debates, 4, 2. *Proceedings and Debates of the Convention of North Carolina,* convened at Hillsboro, etc., 41-42. Printed at Edenton by Hodge & Wills, 1789. This controlling vote has been praised by some Carolinians.

123. Dr. John Manning, William R. Davie, University of North Carolina Magazine, 12, 103. Dr. J. G. deR. Hamilton, "William Richardson Davie", James Sprunt Historial Monograph No. 7, 14.

124. Dr. Kemp P. Battle, History of the University of North Carolina, 1, 5.

125. Dr. Archibald Henderson, *The Old North State and The News,* 1, 400. Chief Justice Walter Clark, "William R. Davie," in W. J. Peele's *Lives of Distinguished North Carolinians,* 71. Same, Preface to Volume XX. The State Records of North Carolina, V, VI.

126. Capt. Samuel A. Ashe, William Richardson Davie, *Biographical History of North Carolina* VI, 193.

127. Same, *History of North Carolina,* 11, 73.

128. Dr. R. D. W. Connor, *North Carolina, Rebuilding an Ancient Commonwealth,* 1, 415, 416.

129. Stephen B. Weeks, *Biographical History of North Carolina* IV, 397.

Hunt & Scott, *Debates in Federal Convention,* 259 note.
130. Blount to Caswell, July 10, N.C.S.R. XX, 734.
131. Blount to Blount, Farrand IV, 71.
132. Farrand II, 15, Hunt & Scott, 259.
133. Farrand II, 223.
134. Washington Irving, *Life of Washington,* Bedford Company Ed. III, 460.
135. N.C.S.R. XX, 766. Farrand, III, 71.
136. Thorpe, III, 466, 467.
137. Farrand, II, 481.
138. Thorpe, III, 466, 467.
139. Warren, 686.
140. Farrand, II, 483 et seq.
141. Thos. B. Reed in "Sketch of Gunning Bedford," Historical and Bio-graphical Papers of Historical Society of Delaware, XXVI.
142. James M. Beck, *The Constitution of the United States,* quoting Robt. Morris, 173. *John Adams.*—"A result of accommodation cannot be supposed to reach the ideas of perfection of any one; but the conception of such an idea and the deliberate union of so great and various a people in such a plan is, without all partiality or prejudice, if not the greatest exertion of human understanding, the greatest single effort of national deliberation that the world has seen." John Adams, A Defense of the Constitution, III, 506. *William E. Gladstone*—"As the British Constitu-tion is the most subtle organism which has proceeded from progressive history, so the American Constitution is the most wonderful work every struck off at a given time by the brain and purpose of man." *Great Debates in American History,* I, 271.
143. Wheeler's *History of N.C.* (1851), 361.
144. George Tayloe Winston, *A Builder of the New South,* quoting, also, stirring statement of Mr. Daniel A. Tompkins.
145. See Note 14.
146. Farrand I, 526, 546. Farrand II, 233.

FOOTNOTES ON SKETCH OF WILLIAM BLOUNT

1. Edmund Cody Burnett, *The Continental Congress,* 673.
2. State Records of North Carolina, XX, 734, 735. (Hereafter N.C.S.R.)
3. N.C.S.R. XX, 734, 735.
4. Burnett, *The Continental Congress,* 692. N.C.S.R. Supra.
5. Burnett, 693. N.C.S.R. XX, 764. Elliot, 1, 362 (Luther Martin defines "Federalist")
6. Max Farrand, *The Records of The Federal Convention* (1937) (hereafter Farrand), II, 646. James M. Beck, *The Constitution of the United States, Yesterday, Today, and Tomorrow,* 167.
7. Farrand, II, 645.
8. Farrand, III, 95.
9. N.C.S.R. XXII, 1 et seq., 36 et seq., 41.
10. Wheeler's *Reminiscences,* LVII, LXI; General Marcus J. Wright, *Life and Services of William Blount,* 10; Theodore Roosevelt, *The Winning of the West,* Vol. 2, 270, 7, 90. McKenzie, *Washington Genealogy,* VII, 348. Hoppin, I, 55. *Dictionary of American Biography* (Blount).
11. Linda Tunstall Rodman, *North Carolina Booklet,* XXII, 49.
12. Ibid, 50.
13. North Carolina Society of the Cincinnati, Past & Present Members, 1940, 6.
14. N.C.S.R. XX, 777, 779.
15. Jeffery's Map, being a Map of Virginia, Maryland, and parts of Pennsylvania, New Jersey and North Carolina, drawn by Joshua Fry, and Peter Jefferson in 1775, including Western Surveys of Christopher Gist, made in 1751, 2, 3, and 4, and showing location of the Gist home on the Yadkin in North Carolina and his trail from Kentucky down to his home, 18 years before Boone's first trip. Don Marshall Larrabee of the Williamsport, Penn. Bar, *A Report of the Journals of George Washington and His Guide, Christopher Gist,* etc. to the French Forts on Lake Erie, in November and December 1753, giving graphic account of their relations, 23, 35, 36. William M. Darlington, *Christopher Gist's* Journals, etc. J. Stoddard Johnston, *First Explorations of Kentucky,* Filson Club Publication No. 13, giving Captain Gist's account of his trip back to North Carolina from Kentucky, 166.
16. Thomas Perkins Abernethy, (hereafter Abernethy), *From Frontier to Plantation in Tennessee,* 80, 65, 66, 75.
17. It is said that about 50% of the North Carolina lands in the Great Smoky Mountain Park trace back to John Gray Blount's grants. Letter to writer from H. C. Welbourn, Superintendent of the Park. Justice George H. Brown, 116 N.C.Rep. (Ann.Ed.) 631 ff.
18. Abernethy, 53, 128, 129. Joshua W. Caldwell, *Studies in the Constitutional History of Tennessee,* 88 (4 horse fellows). Samuel Cole Williams, *History*

of the Lost State of Franklin, Chapter III, The Great Bend of the Tennessee, 13.

19. St. George Leakin Sioussat, *The North Carolina Session Act of 1784, in its Federal Aspects* (Pamphlet) 9, 10, 15, 16, 17. Samuel Cole Williams, *Lost State of Franklin,* Chapter IV, 18, 22.

20. Theodore Roosevelt, *The Winning of the West,* 349-50 (hereafter Roosevelt).

21. Albert V. Goodpasture, "William Blount and the Old Southwest Territory," in the American Historical Magazine and Tennessee Quarterly, VIII, No. I, January, 1903 (hereafter Goodpasture). Clarence Edwin Carter, (hereafter Carter), *The Territory South of the River Ohio,* (1790-1796), being Vol. IV of the Territorial Papers of the United States, 18, 19-23, 24, 21, n. 39, 30. N.C.S.R. XVIII, 767. Roosevelt, 2, 360, 361, 362.

22. Carter, supra, *Papers on Southwest Territory,* 24, n. 46.

23. Archibald Henderson, *Washington's Southern Tour,* 1791, 6, 7, 8, 78 (Should be Thomas), 82.

24. Roosevelt, 2, 353 ff. Albert Bushnell Heart, of Harvard, quoted by Miss Mary Boyce Temple in Pamphlet of the Governor Blount Mansion Association, First Entrance of Women in Higher Institutions of Learning in the United States. United States Supreme Court Justice Edward T. Sanford, *Blount College and the University of Tennessee,* 6, 11, 13, 23, An Historical Address, published by the University of Tennessee.

25. Carter supra, 60-66. Goodpasture, supra, pamphlet. Abernethy, 53. Col. Benjamin Hawkin's *Sketch of the Creek Country,* In Collections of the Georgia Historical Society, Roosevelt, *The Winning of the West,* 2, 363.

26. J.F.D. Smyth, *A Tour in the United States of America,* etc. 1-p. 247. Obituary of Jacob Blount written by Judge Sitgreaves and Richard Dobbs Spaight; Published in the *STATE GAZETTE OF NORTH CAROLINA,* August 20, 1789; Copy furnished the writer by Miss Alice B. Keith of the Department of History, Meredith College, N.C.: Died on Monday the 17th instant, of a nervous fever, at his seat Blount Hall, Col. Jacob Blount, aged 63 years — He was possessed of an affluent fortune, which he acquired by his own industry, in the early part of his life, and enjoyed in the latter part of his life, with use and liberality; in either of which he never risked his good name, but on the contrary enhanced it — independent in his sentiments, and steady in his resolutions, he obeyed the impulse of his own mind — by always doing that which appeared to him right, obtained the friendship of many, and the esteem and respect of all who knew him. It would be difficult to determine whether his hospitality was most general or liberal — at all times his doors were alike open to the poor and the rich — the distressed, the weary, and the sick traveller were sure to find a home at Blount Hall; and the face of honesty was the best recommendation there

— in public life he was the real patriot, in private, the uniform, steady and sincere friend; he adjusted the differences in his neighborhood with justice and moderation and contributed much to the order, peace, and happiness of it — he was candid, cheerful, and social — seldom too grave for the young, or too gay for the old; the equality of his spirits bespoke the comforts of a quiet conscience, and agreeable to the idea of Pope, he was "the noblest work of God — an HONEST MAN."

27. J.G.M. Ramsey, M.D., *The Annals of Tennessee*, (hereafter Ramsey) 54, et. seq. 546-47, John P., Brown, *Old Frontiers*, (1938), is a definitive account of the Cherokee Indians and the troubles with them and others during the days of the Southwest Territory.

28. Goodpasture, 10. Abernethy, 92, 135 ff. Caldwell, 83 ff. Ramsey, Chap. VIII, 647. Edward T. Sanford, *Constitutional Convention of 1796*, (pamphlet), 11, 12, 15.

29. Edmund C. Burnett, *Letters of Members of the Continental Congress*, VIII, 585. Goodpasture, 11. Abernethy, 142.

30. James Truslow Adams, *Dictionary of American History*, (1940) (hereafter Adams), IV, 272. Ibid, III, 169 (Jay Treaty). Ibid, IV, 272. Ibid, V, 316. William L. Langer, *An Encyclopedia of World History* (1940) 774, 775.

31. Bartlett, *Familiar Quotations* (9th Ed.) 673. Chas. A. & Mary R. Beard, *The Rise of American Civilization*, (New Ed. 2 vols. in 1) 394 ff. Appleton's *Encyc of Am. Biog.* V, 22. Adams, III, 304. Ibid, V, 24. Langer, 774, 457.

32. Adams, III, 426.

33. Willie Blount, *William Blount's Vindication*. (See Henderson note 35.)

34. General Marcus J. Wright, *Life & Services of William Blount*, 5, 181.

35. Archibald Henderson, discussing letter of Willie Blount, North Carolina Daily Papers, May 20, 1928. Ramsey, 702. Goodpasture, supra, 12. Wright, supra, caps, XXVII, XXXIII, XXIV, XXX, 105 ff, 111.

36. Wright, supra, 138, 111.

37. Roosevelt, 2, 431. Among other things he said (351): "In consequence he speedily became a man of great influence for good. The Secretary of the Territory reported to the Federal Government that the effect of Blount's character on the frontiersmen was far greater than was the case of any other man and that he was able to get them to adhere to the principles of order and to support the laws by his influence in a way which it was hopeless to expect from their own respect for government authority. Blount was felt by the frontiersmen to be thoroughly in sympathy with them, to understand and appreciate them and to be heartily anxious for their welfare; and yet at the same time his influence could be counted upon on the side of Order, which the majority of the frontier officials in any time of commotion were apt to remain silent and inactive or even to express

their sympathy with the disorderly element. No one but a man of great tact and firmness could have preserved as much order among the frontiersmen as Blount preserved. He was always under fire from both sides. The settlers were continually complaining that they were deserted by the Federal authorities who favored the Indians and that Blount himself did not take sufficiently active steps to subdue the savages while on the other hand, the National Administration was continually upbraiding him for being too active against the Indians and for not keeping the frontiersmen sufficiently peaceful." Also: Story, 2, 267; Ramsey, 702; Wright, 111-112.

38. Joseph Gales, (printer) *Proceedings on the Impeachment of William Blount,* 21-101, 102, Wright, supra, also Ramsey, 699 ff.
39. *Jefferson's Complete Works,* Taylor & Maury Publishers, (1883), Vol. 4, 432. Bernard Mayo, *Jefferson Himself,* 241, Chap. XIII. John T. Morse, *American Statesmen* Series Volume XI, Thomas Jefferson, 210 et seq.
40. Adams, V, 134 (2d. col.) Claude G. Bowers, *Jefferson in Power,* 210.
41. Gales, supra, 20, 21 (note). Wright, 132 ff. Ramsey, 699 ff. (Crockett) Dr. Ernest L. Stockton p. 25 (See note 44 infra).
42. Roosevelt, 2, 352.
43. Ramsey, 541, 542.
44. Dr. Ernest L. Stockton, Pres., Cumberland University, Tenn., "History Excursions into Tennessee, Its Early Hermitage," (1941) p. 26, being a Newcomen Address at Union League Club, N.Y. 11/19/40.
45. Abernethy, 168.
46. Samuel Cole Williams, *Early Travels in the Tennessee Country,* 522, 458, 459, n-32, n-33.
47. Fred Taylor Wilson, *The Constitution and Its Makers,* 490. Wright, 197.
48. Wright, 142.

See also:
    Abernethy, 168
    Brown, 307, 308, & Index
    Caldwell, 83, 84, 85, 88.
    Goodpasture, 12, 13.
    Phelan, 148.
    Ramsey, 702.
    Roosevelt, 2, Caps. IX, XII, XIII.
    Sanford, 6, 11, 13, 23.
    Wright, Life & Services.

FOOTNOTES ON SKETCH OF ALEXANDER MARTIN

1. Francis Nash, Esq., Presentatin of a Portrait of Governor Alexander Martin to the State of North Carolina by the North Carolina Society of the Sons of the Revolution. (hereafter Nash) Justice Robert M. Douglas, Alexander Martin, *Biographical History of North Carolina*, III, 274.
2. Nash, 4.
3. Nash, 5.
4. Henry Cabot Lodge, Address at unveiling Statue of John C. Calhoun in Statuary Hall, Washington, D.C. 33.
5. Irving Brant, *James Madison, the Virginia Revolutionist*, 57, 65, 67. (hereafter Brant)
6. Brant, 82.
7. Brant, 71.
8. Brant, 122, 123. Nash, 18.
9. *Salisbury Watchman*, Nov. 18, 1834, Account of his death and services.
10. Colonial Records of North Carolina, VI, 1077. Colonial Records, VII, 277 (a justice of the peace 1766).
11. Office of the Clerk of Superior Court of Rowan County, Salisbury, N.C.
12. Samuel J. Erwin, Jr., *A Colonial History of Rowan County, North Carolina*, 23. (See James Sprunt Historical Publications, 16, No. 1.) N.C.S.R., XXIII, 810, 813. Colonial Records, IX, 318 (Appears as surety for Clerk of Court, Adlai Osborne, 1772.)
13. Rumple's *History of Rowan County*, Article by Hon. John S. Henderson on Episcopacy in Rowan County, 389. Col. Rec., IX, 673-5. Col. Rec., X, 1, Transcript of Minutes of a Court of Oyer & Terminer for Salisbury District composed of Counties of Rowan, Anson, Mecklenburg, Tryon, Surry and Guilford, showing Hon. Alexander Martin, Esq. took oath of office, etc. at Salisbury, as one of the Judges, June 1st, 1775. Col. Rec., 10-953. (Allowed pay as Judge) John S. Bassett, *The Regulators of North Carolina*, 200, See Note 17 infra. Col. Rec., VIII, 521-2, (Agreement with Regulators)
14. Nash, 5, 6. Brant, 71.
15. Nash, 6.
16. Col. Rec., VIII, 533-36, Alexander Martin and John Frobock to Governor Tryon. Col. Rec., VIII, 545, Governor Tryon's Reply.
17. John S. Bassett, "The Regulators of North Carolina," Annual Report of the American Historical Association, (1894), 141, 191, (best account). R.D.W. Connor, *History of North Carolina*, I, 314. Wm. Henry Foote, Sketches of North Carolina, 60.
18. Col. Records, X, 187. Col. Records, X, 482. Col. Records, X, 468. Col. Records, X, 408 (Scovellites). Col. Records, X, (preface), XI, XII. Col. Records, X, 136, Commended by Committee of Safety, on Dunn and Boote matter.

19. Col. Records, X, 495. R.D.W. Connor, *History of No. Car.* I, 440. Col. Records, X, (preface) XXXIX.
20. N.C.S.R., XI, 677. N.C.S.R., XI, 694. N.C.S.R., XI, 654. N.C.S.R., XIII, 262-4, (His own letter to Governor Caswell). Nash, 10.
21. Board of War, N.C.S.R., XIV, 376. Council Extraordinary, Nash, 12. Cincinnati, N.C.S.R., XII, 911.
22. N.C.S.R., XVII, 312, 339, 342. N.C.S.R., XX, 30, 57. N.C.S.R., XXIV, 779 (Town laid off at Guilford Court House.)
23. Nash, 9.
24. R.D.W. Connor, *North Carolina Manual* (1913), 399, 630, 631, 454, 455, 456, 784, 461, 417, Bronze marker in front of Salem College.
25. Connor, Manual (1913), 417. N.C.S.R., XVI, 958-9. Chief Justice Clark's estimate, N.C.S.R., XVII (preface) III, IV. N.C.S.R., XIX, (preface) III, IV, (also Clarke's estimate).
26. N.C.S.R., XVII, (preface) III, IV. N.C.S.R., XXI (preface), V. Chas. L. Coon, *The Beginning of Public Education in North Carolina,* I, 53-56, Publications of North Carolina Historical Commission. N.C.S.R., XIX, 492, 494-99. Nash, 16.
27. N.C.S.R., XXIV, 250, Hillsboro. N.C.S.R., XXIV, 690, Salisbury. N.C.S.R., XXIV, 754, Kinston.
28. N.C.S.R., XXIV, 536. Justice Edward T. Sanford, *Blount College and The University of Tennessee,* 9.
29. These schools were established in Rowan before the counties (Iredell and Guilford) into which three of them subsequently fell, were cut off Rowan.
30. N.C.S.R., XXI, 974-5. Nash, 16.
31. Farrand, III, 55. (Clark, C.J.) N.C.S.R., XVIII, (preface) III & IV. N.C.S.R., XIX. (preface) III. (Thanked) N.C.S.R., XVII, 177. N.C.S.R. XVII, 422, 423. N.C.S.R., XIX, 170. N.C.S.R. XX, 115, 117. N.C.S.R., XXII, 54, (and elsewhere).
32. Farrand, III, 71, 72. N.C.S.R., XX, 763-5. Farand, III, 589.
33. Elliot's *Debates* 5, 292, 230, 374.
34. Chas. Warren, *The Making of the Constitution,* 303.
35. Nash, 16, Governor Martin's Address to The General Assembly Dec. 22, 1789, in advocacy of the New Constitution.
36. Robert M. Douglass, *Biographical History of North Carolina,* III, 279.
37. Same. Justice Douglass says that no other governor has had such a record.
38. Elizabeth Winston Yates. Theses for Degree of Master of Arts, University of North Carolina, 1943.

FOOTNOTES ON SKETCH
OF WILLIAM RICHARDSON DAVIE

1. Farrand, I, 520.
4. Chapter I, herein.
5. Chapter I, herein.
6. Farrand, II, 15.
7. Farrand I, 605.
8. Farrand, I, 229; I, 243; I, 526.
9. Farrand, I, 593.
10. Farrand, III, Appendix A, CLXX, 255.
11. Farrand, I, 78; II, 64.
12. Farrand, I, 542.
13. Farrand, III, 4, 71; III, 55; III, 70; III, 90.
14. *Proceedings and Debates of the Convention of North Carolina,* convened at Hillsboro, on Monday, the 21st day of July, 1788, for deliberating and determining on the Constitution recommended by the General Convention at Philadelphia, the 17th day of September, 1787. Edenton. Published by Hodge & Wills, Printers to the State, M, DCC, LXXXIX — 18, 19, 28, 32, 33. Reprinted in Elliott's Debates, 4, 1 et seq.
15. *Convention of North Carolina,* 1788, above, 36; Elliott, 4, 16, and following pages.
16. At page 254, of *Proceedings and Debates,* Note 14 Supra, Mr. Willie Jones, on Thursday, July 31, just before Saturday, August 2, 1788, when his resolution neither to ratify nor reject passed by a large majority, told the Convention of an unheeded letter from Mr. Jefferson to Mr. Madison, while the Virginia Convention was sitting in Richmond, saying that he wished nine states would adopt the Constitution, etc; but that he wished the other four would reject it, so that there might be a certainty of obtaining amendments. No doubt, the North Carolina Convention's mind was already fixed and many of its members already familiar with Mr. Jefferson's views. He failed to tell the Convention of the movement already afoot by the adopting states, including Virginia, to incorporate the Bill of Rights. When North Carolina "caught on," she adopted the Constitution on November 21, 1789, just in time to have a hand in accepting the amendments. On July 31, 1788, after the necessary ninth state, New Hampshire, had ratified on June 21, Virginia on June 26, and New York on July 26, 1788, Mr. Jefferson wrote Mr. Madison that he sincerely rejoiced at the acceptance of the Constitution. This left only North Carolina and Rhode Island out in the raw cold. General Davie, at least, had too much information and sense to follow such leadership. Archibald Henderson, *North Carolina,* 1, 599, on Iredell-Davie address.
17. N.C.S.R. XXII, 41, 42, 48.

18. Fordyce M. Hubbard, *William Richardson Davie*, in *Library of American Biography*, by Jared Sparks, XV, 3, et seq. John H. Wheeler, *Historical Sketches of North Carolina*, II, 188 (Reprint). C. L. Hunter, *Sketches of Western Carolina*, 99, et seq. Walter Clark, William R. Davie, in *Lives of Distinguished North Carolinians* by W. J. Peale, 59, et seq. Samuel A. Ashe, William Richardson Davie, in *Biographical History of North Carolina*, VI, 188. Rev. Jethro Rumple, *History of Rowan County*, 137-140, 197 (Reprint).

19. Lily Doyle Dunlap, "Old Waxhaw," The North Carolina Booklet, XX, 139. Robert Ney McNeely, "Union County and Old Waxhaw Settlement," *The North Carolina Booklet*, XII, 6, 10.

20. Professor Walter Lincoln Whittlesey, *The Story of a Fighting Pedagogue*, The Princeton Alumni Weekly, June 7, 1929, 1055. Dr. John Witherspoon's Certificate, N.C.S.R. IX, 870.

21. Dr. Jethro Rumple in his *History of Rowan County*, says Col. Davie's Troop of Cavalry was raised in Rowan County, 137-140, 197 (Reprint), with which he and "his Rowan Boys" made a brilliant display of courage.

22. His licenses are framed and hung on the walls of the old Supreme Court rooms in Raleigh. N.C.S.R., XV, 385, 386.

23. Chief Justice Clark, supra, (Jackson) 62, (personal combats) 65, quoting Gardner's Anecdotes of the Revolution. (Rebellious Tract) Lord Cornwallis's answer to General Clinton's narrative, being his dispatch No. 7, to Lord George Germain dated at Guilford, March 17, 1781. (Maj. General) Ashe, 194.

24. Chief Justice Clark, above, 70.

25. Same.

26. "Revolutionary History of North Carolina, in Three Lectures, etc.", compiled by Wm. S. Cooke, A.M. 224, John Penn is doubtless John Dunn. See 233. Court Records, Clerk's Office, Rowan County. N.C.S.R., XVI, 523. Colonel Samuel Bryan has been said to have been an ancestor of William Jennings Bryan.

27. 12 *Corpus Juris*, 778, giving in chronological order a list of early American cases, including *Byard v. Singleton*. James Brown Scott, *James Madison's Notes*, etc. and A Society of Nations, 64.

28. Capt. Ashe, supra, 193. Chief Justice Clark, supra, 70.

29. Clark, above, 72.

30. Nearly every writer on his life.

31. Rev. Jethro Rumple, supra, 197. N.C.S.R. 22, 25.

32. Chief Justice Clark, Peele's Sketches, 73. Daniel L. Grant, Catalogue University of N.C. (1926), 748.

33. Clark, above, 75 following.

34. Ashe, above, 195.

35. Clark, above, 76, 77. Ashe, above, 195.
36. Wheeler, above, 198.
37. Clarke, above, 80.
38. Clarke, above, 79.

FOOTNOTES ON SKETCH
OF RICHARD DOBBS SPAIGHT

1. Jonathan Elliott, *Debates on the Adoption of the Federal Constitution,* (hereafter Elliot) 5, Index, (1845) (1854), 636. Max Farrand, *The Records of the Federal Convention of 1787,* (hereafter Farrand) IV, Index, 216.
2. Farrand, I, 9, 10.
3. Farrand, I, 36.
4. Farrand, II, 15. Elliot, 5, 316. Hunt & Scott, *Debates in the Federal Convention,* 259, note.
5. Farrand, II, 665.
6. Farrand, II, 525.
7. Farrand, II, 95, 99, 515, 525, 526.
8. Farrand, I, 218, 525.
9. Farrand, I, 218.
10. Farrand, I, 390.
11. Farrand, I, 51, 52.
12. Same.
13. Farrand, II, 540.
14. Farrand, II, 261.
15. Farrand, II, 543.
16. Farrand, II, 451.
17. James Franklin Jameson, *Studies in the History of the Federal Convention of 1787,* 100.
18. Warren, 134, 131.
19. N.C.S. Records XX, 752. See also N.C.S.R. XX, 753.
20. McRee's *Iredell,* II, 168.
21. McRee's *Iredell,* II, 169 et seq.

Philadelphia
August 12, 1787

Dear Sir:

****

The late determination of our judges at Newbern, must, in my opinion, produce the most serious reflections in the breast of every thinking man, and of every well-wisher to his country. It cannot be denied, but that the Assembly have passed laws unjust in themselves, and militating in their principles against the Constitution, in more instances than one, and in my opinion of a more alarming and destructive nature than the one which the judges by their own authority, thought proper to set aside and declare void. . . . I do not pretend to vindicate the law, which has been the subject of controversy: it is immaterial what law they have declared void; it is their unsurpation of the authority to do it, that I complain of, as I do most positively deny that they have any such power; nor can they find anything in the Constitution, either directly or impliedly, that will support them, or give them any color of right to exercise that authority. Besides, it would have been absurd, and contrary to the practice of all the world, had the Constitution vested such powers in them, as they would have operated as an absolute negative on the proceedings of the Legislature, which no judiciary ought ever to possess: and the State, instead of being governed by the representatives in general Assembly, would be subject to the will of three individuals, who united in their own persons the legislative and judiciary powers, which no monarch in Europe enjoys, and which would be more despotic than the Roman Decemvirate, and equally as insufferable. If they possessed the power, what check or control would there be to their proceedings? or who is there to take the same liberty with them, that they have taken with the Legislature, and declare their opinions to be erroneous? none that I know of. In consequence of which, whenever the judges should become corrupt, they might at pleasure set aside every law, however, just or consistent with the Constitution, to answer their designs; and the persons and property of every individual would be completely at their disposal. Many instances might be brought to show the absurdity and impropriety of such a power being lodged with the judges.

It must be acknowledged that our Constitution, unfortunately, has not provided a sufficient check, to prevent the intemperate and unjust proceedings of our Legislature, though such a check would be very beneficial, and, I think, absolutely necessary to our well-being; the only one that I know of, is the annual election, which by leaving out such members as have supported improper measures, will in some degree remedy, though it cannot prevent, such evils as may arise. I should not have intruded this subject upon you, but as it must certainly undergo a public discussion, I wish to know what is the general opinion on that transaction.

****

RICH'D DOBBS SPAIGHT

22. J. B. Scott, *James Madison's Notes* and a Society of Nations, 64. Hannis Taylor, *The Origin & Growth of the English Constitution,* 1, 80.
23. McRee's *Iredell,* Vol. II, 172. On August 16, 1786, Judge Iredell published an address to the Public in the New Bern paper, on this subject. Taylor, above, 1, 80.

August 26th, 1787

Dear Sir:

****

In regard to the late decision at Newbern, I confess it has ever been my opinion, that an act inconsistent with the Constitution was void; and that the judges, consistently with their duties, could not carry it into effect. The Constitution appears to me to be a fundamental law, limiting the powers of the Legislature, and with which every exercise of those powers must, necessarily, be compared. Without an express Constitution the powers of the Legislature would undoubtedly have been absolute (as the Parliament in Great Britain is held to be), and any act passed, not *inconsistent with natural justice* (for that curb is avowed by the judges even in England), would have been binding on the people. The experience of the evils which the American war fully disclosed, attending an absolute power in a legislative body, suggested the propriety of a real, original contract between the people and their future Government, such, perhaps, as there has been no instance of in the world but in America. Had not this been the case, bills of attainder, and other acts of party violence, might have ruined many worthy individuals here, as they have frequently done in England, where such things are much oftener the acts of a party than the result of a fair judicial enquiry. In a republican Government (as I conceive), *individual liberty* is a matter of the utmost moment, as, if there be no check upon the public passions, it is in the greatest danger. The majority having the rule in their own hands, may take care of themselves; but in what condition are the minority, if the power of the other is without limit? These considerations, I suppose, or similar ones, occasioned such express provisions for the personal liberty of each citizen, which the citizens, when they formed the Constitution, chose to reserve as an unalienated right, and not to leave at the mercy of any Assembly whatever. The restriction might be attended with inconvenience; but they chose to risk the inconvenience, for the sake of the advantage; and in every transaction we must act in the same manner: we must choose between evils of some sort or other: the imperfection of man can never keep entirely clear of all. The Constitution, therefore, being a *fundamental law* and a law *in writing* of the solemn nature I have mentioned (which is the light in which it strikes me), the judicial power, in the exercise of their authority, must take notice of it as the groundwork of that as well as of all other authority; and as no article of the Constitution can be repealed by a Legislature, which derives its whole power from it, it follows either that the *fundamental unrepealable* law must be obeyed, by the rejection of an act unwarranted by and inconsistent with it, or you must obey an act founded on an authority not given by the people, and to which, therefore, the people owe no obedience. It is not that the judges are appointed arbiters, and to determine as it were upon any application, whether the Assembly have or have not violated the Constitution; but when an act is necessarily brought in judgment before them, they must unavoidably, determine one way or another. . . . Suppose, therefore, the Assembly should pass an act, declaring that in future in all criminal trials the trial by jury should be abolished, and the court alone should determine. The Attorney-General indicts; the indictment is found; the criminal is arraigned, and the Attorney-General requires his trial to come on. The Criminal objects, alleging that by the Constitution all the citizens in such cases are entitled to a trial by jury; and that the Assembly have no right to alter any part of the Constitution; and that therefore the act appointing the trial by the court is void. Must not the court determine some way or other, whether the man shall be tried or not? Must not they say whether they will obey the Constitution or an act inconsistent with it? . . . . It really appears to me, the exercise of the power is unavoidable, the Constitution not being a mere imaginary thing, about which ten thousand different opinions may be formed, but a written document to which all may have recourse, and to which, therefore, the judges cannot wilfully blind themselves. . . . In any other light than I have stated it, the greater part of the provisions of the Constitution would appear to me to be ridiculous, since in my opinion nothing could be more so than for the representatives of a people solemnly assembled to form a Constitution, to set down a number of political dogmas, which might or might not be regarded; whereas it must have been intended, as I conceive, that it should be a system of authority, not depending on the casual whim or accidental ideas of a majority either in or out of doors for the time being; but to remain in force until by a similar appointment of deputies specially appointed for the same important purpose; and alterations should be with equal solemnity and deliberation made. And this, I apprehend, must be the necessary consequence, since surely equal authority is required to repeal as to enact. That such a power in the Judge may be abused is very certain; that it *will* be, is not very probable. . . . so that it really seems to me, the danger is the most chimerical that can be supposed of this power being abused; and if you had seen as I did, with what infinite reluctance the judges came to this decision, what pains they took by proposing expedients to obviate its necessity, you would have seen in a strong light how little probably it is a judge would ever give such a judgment, where he thought he could possibly avoid it. But whatever may be the consequence, formed as our Constitution is, I cannot help thinking they are not at liberty to choose, but must in all questionable instances decide upon it. It is a subject indeed of great magnitude, and I heartily lament the occasion for its discussion. In all doubtful cases, to be sure, the Act ought to be supported: it should be unconstitutional beyond dispute before it is pronounced such.

James Iredell

24. Elliot, 5, 128.
25. Elliot, 5, 151.
26. Elliot, 5, 151.
27. Elliot, 5, 344.
28. Elliot, 5, 355-356. Warren, 350.
29. Elliot, 5, 348.
30. Elliot, 5, 346-7. Elliot, 1, 380. *Martin of Maryland* also discusses Judicial Power in his letter of Jan. 27, 1788, to the speaker of the House of Delegates of Maryland.
31. Elliot, 5, 349.
32. Elliot, 5, 429.
33. Elliot, 5, 463. Warren, 502.
34. Warren, 337.
35. Warren, 245. Elliot, 5, 321.
36. Warren, 248, Note I, and, generally, 320, 323, 331, et seq. 434-435, 350.
37. Elliot, 4, 136-139, 139.
38. Farrand, II, 186.
39. Warren, 541, 544, Farrand, II, 431.
40. Farrand, II, 428, Warren, 531.
41. Farrand, II, 430, Warren, 538, 539.
42. Constitution of the United States, Art. VI, Clause 2, Farrand, II, 662. Woodrow Wilson, *Constitutional Government In the United States,* 156, 157. Dr. Hugh Williamson, first good expression as to this thought, FARRAND, 1, 207. As to the Articles of Confederation, see *Bayard v. Singleton* case.
43. Farrand, III, 63. J. B. Scott, *James Madison's Notes and a Society of Nations,* 74, 75.
44. Same — 76.
45. Articles of Confederation, Art. IX, where the procedure is outlined. Hunt & Scott, XLI.
46. Farrand, II, 186, being Art. XI, sec. 3.
47. Farrand, II, 400, 401.
48. Same, 401.
49. Farrand, II, 600, being Article III, Section 2. Warren, 544.
50. N.C.S.R. XX, 729, Farrand, III, 52.
51. Raleigh Register, February 28, 1852.
52. Farrand, III, 95. All of the North Carolina letters readily may be found in the excellent COLONIAL AND STATE RECORDS OF NORTH CAR-

OLINA with their index and some of them in LETTERS OF MEMBERS OF THE CONTINENTAL CONGRESS by Edmund Cody Burnett. They are also discussed by James Franklin Jameson in STUDIES IN THE HISTORY OF THE FEDERAL CONVENTION and by Burnett in THE CONTINENTAL CONGRESS. There is an interesting letter from the delegates then present, on June 14, 1787, to Governor Caswell, on the general progress of the Convention and another at the close of it, on September 18, giving their impressions at length on how North Carolina had been fairly treated. N.C.S.R. XX, 723-4 and 777-9.

53. Elliot 4. Farrand, III, 342, 343, 345, 346, 349, 351, 352. *Proceedings in the Hillsboro Convention 1788*, reported by Iredell and Davie and printed in Edenton by Hodge and Wills, 1789 (rare).

54. Elliot, 4, 206-10.

55. Elliot, 4, 27.

56. Farrand, III, 343.

57. Elliot, 4, 82.

58. Elliot, 4, 100.

59. Elliot, 4, 101.

60. Elliot, 4, 104, 105.

61. Elliot, 4, 114, 115.

62. Elliot, 4, 144.

63. Farrand, III, 349.

64. Elliot, 4, 136-139.

65. Alexander B. Andrews, "Richard Dobbs Spaight," *The North Carolina Historical Review* 1, 95. Stephen B. Weeks, Richard Dobbs Spaight, Sr., *Biographical History of North Carolina* IV, 397. He erroneously gives Spaight credit for change in North Carolina's vote.

66. Andrews, above. Ellis, Henry, *A Voyage to Hudson Bay the Dobb's Galley,* etc., for discovery of a Northwest passage, to which Arthur Dobbs and Rev. Richard Dobbs were both subscribers. Dr. J. DeR. Hamilton, Vol. V Dictionary of American Biography, 336.

67. Andrews.

68. Andrews.

68a. Free incorporation under general law. Commencement address of Hon. Simeon Eben Baldwin at Wake Forest College in May 1914, on *Contribution of North Carolina to the Development of American Institutions.* Reported in North Carolina Booklet XIV, 141 et seq. Anglo-American Legal History Vol. III, 250, Note 1, William Meade Fletcher, Cyclopedia of the Law of Private Corporations. Vol. 1, 8, 9.

69. Andrews, with citations to N.C.S.R. XVIII, 194, 213, 348, 400, 425, 428.

70. N.C.S.R. XX, 706, 707.

71. Edmund Cody Burnett, *The Continental Congress,* 558-559. *Biographical*

Directory of the American Congress (1774-1912), 35.

72.   Hannis Taylor, *The Origin & Growth of the American Constitution*, 256-7.

73. Burnett, 625.

74. Burnett, 625-626.

75. Burnett, 609-11, Cap. XXX 593 et seq.

76. Burnett, 590-591. (1783).

77. Connor, *North Carolina Manual 1913*, 417. Samuel A. Ashe, History of North Carolina II, Cap. IX, 134-147.

78. Ashe, above.

79. Andrews, above, 113-114.

80. Col. John W. Wheeler, *Reminiscences*, 135.

81. Andrews, 112.

FOOTNOTES ON SKETCH OF DR. HUGH WILLIAMSON

1. David Hosack, M.D. LL.D., "A Biographical Memoir of Hugh William-son, M.D., LL.D." (1820) p. 50 et seq. He was an eminent scientist and physician of New York and a friend of Dr. Williamson for 25 years and his memoir is one of the chief sources of information on the Doctor's life. Carl Van Doren, *Benjamin Franklin,* 442-3, indicating Franklin's letter trans-mitting Hutchison's Letters, December 2, 1772. Colonel John W. Wheeler, *Historical Sketches of North Carolina,* (Reprint Edition) 91. Stephen B. Weeks, *Biographical History of North Carolina* V, 458. Delbert Harold Gilpatrick, "Contemporary Opinion of Hugh Williamson," *The North Carolina Historial Review* XVIII, No. 1, 26-36. John W. Francis, an eminent New York physician) *Old New York, or Reminiscences of the past Sixty years.* Louise Irby Trenholme, Ph.D., *The Ratification of the Federal Constitution in North Carolina.* Index 281, under Williamson. For list of his publications see sketch of Dr. Williamson by Dr. J. deRoulhac Hamilton in *Dictionary of American Biography.*
2. Griffith J. McRee, *Life and Correspondence of James Iredell,* Vol. 1, pages 32 and following.
3. Phillips Russell, *John Paul Jones, Man of Action,* Chapter VII, 49, 56. Familiar Letters of John Adams and His Wife, No. 189, 282.
4. N.C.S.R. XV, 166-170; XXII, 530-32.
5. Jonathan Elliot, Supplement to Elliot's Debates 5, 44 (Footnote).
6. Edward Cody Burnett, *The Continental Congress,* 480. N.C.S.R. XVI, 882-889, 886.
7. St. George Leakin Siussat of the University of the South (Sewanee). "The North Carolina Cession of 1784 in its Federal Aspects," p. 20, an excellent discussion.
8. Farrand 1, 579. *Biograhical Directory of the American Congress* (1774-1927), 39.
9. Farrand, IV, Index 227-228. Elliot, 5, Index 639. Farrand II, 73.
10. Farrand I, 140, 301, 585, 586. Elliot, 5, 241. Farrand I, 409.
11. Elliot 5, 505. Farrand, 11, 490.
12. Elliot, 5, 149. Farrand I, 88.
13. Farrand I, 229, 243, 580-83, 560. Farrand II, 307, 360, 366, 373, 410, 414, Note, 415. Farrand III, 83, 84, 363. Elliott, 5, 296.
14. Farrand I, 207.
15. Julian Parks Boyd, "A North Carolina Citizen on the Federal Constitu-tion," January 1939 issue of the *North Carolina Historical Review,* p. 40.
16. Charles Warren, *The Making of the Constitution,* p. 302. Max Farrand, *The Records of the Federal Convention* of 1787 (1937), III, 58, 59.
17. Ernest Earnest, *John and William Bartram,* 163 (1940).
18. Farrand III, 95. Colonel John H. Wheeler, *Historical Sketches,* 93. (Reprint)

19. Farrand III, 237. Faint Praise, but says had influence. Delbert Harold Gilpatrick, Contemporary Opinion of Hugh Williamson, 33.
20. Farrand III, 238.
21. Trenholme, 193.McRee's *Iredell*, II, 241-242.
22. Elliot, 4, 239.
23. N.C.S.R. XX. 538, 544, 591. Tyler, Moses Coit, *Patrick Henry, American Statesmen* III 330-354.
24. N.C.S.R. XXII, 41, 42.
25. *Biographical Directory of the American Congress,* 1774-1927, 31, 35.
26. N.C.S.R. XXI, 465.
27. N.C.S.R. XXI, 476.
28. N.C.S.R. XXI, 534; XXI, 495. Trenholme, 217. Burnett, *The Continental Congress,* 724.
29. N.C.S.R. XXI, 485, 486.
30. Elliot, 4, 223. N.C.S.R. XXI, 501-2. Gov. Johnston's letter of Sept. 22, 1788. Burnett, 716 (North Carolina and Rhode Island.)
31. N.C.S.R. XXI, 526. Gov. Johnston's letter of Feb. 19, 1789.
32. N.C.S.R. XXI, 533.
33. N.C.S.R. XXI, 552-552 (Considered himself member of Congress). Trenholme, 231.
34. N.C.S.R. XXI, 552-553; 563, 564.
35. N.C.S.R. XXI, 541, 542.
36. Trenholme, 216.
37. N.C.S.R. XXI, 519, 526, 533-4, 538-539, 552-3, 560-1. On Board of Treasury, Trenholme, 220.
38. University Trustee. N.C.S.R. XXV, 22. N.C.S.R. XXII, 792-4; 795-8.
39. Henry Cabot Lodge, *Alexander Hamilton,* 121. N.C.S.R., XXII, 792-3.
40. Ibid.
41. Hosack, 84.
42. Gilpatrick, *Contemporary Opinion of Hugh Williamson.* 31.
43. N.C.S.R. XX, 766. Farrand III, 71.
44. Potter's Revisal, Vol. 1, p. 789, being Chap. 432, Laws of 1795. Simeon Eben Baldwin, *History of the law of Private Corporations in the Colonies and States,* Vol. III. Select Essays in Anglo-American History; also, North Carolina Booklet, Vol. XIV. No. 3, Jan. 1915, his address at Wake Forest Commencement, where he says this act was the first.
45. Dr. Hosack. *The Columbia Encyclopedia,* under Williamson. See list of his publication in Dr. Hamilton's sketch of Dr. Williamson in *Dictionary of American Biography.*
46. Washington Irving, *Life of Washington,* Vol. III, Appendix I, *Portraits of Washington,* p. 460. (Belford Company Publishers).

ABEL BUELL AND HIS MAP

This rare map was the first American map of the United States printed in our country. There exists today four known copies, and the one reproduced here is the most recently discovered, now in the possession of the New Jersey State Historical Society. The overall size of the original map is 41 by 46 inches. Shortly after the Treaty of Paris, there appeared in 1784 in a little weekly newspaper called the *Connecticut Journal,* published in New Haven, the following notice:

Buels' Map

of the United States of America, laid down from the latest observations and best authorities, agreeable to the peace of 1783, is now published and ready for subscribers.

As this map is the effect of the compiler's long and unwearied application, diligence and industry, and as perfection has been the great object of his labours, and it being the first ever compiled, engraved and finished by one man, and an American, he flatters himself, that every patriotic gentleman, and lover of geographical knowledge, will not hesitate to encourage the improvement of his own country. Every favour will be most gratefully acknowledged by the public's most obedient and very humble servant,

Abel Buel

And who was Abel Buell? A most remarkable person, typical of Yankee ingenuity, who saw the need of producing such a map, and accomplished this feat in a manner not the least unusual for his time — by copying other pre-revolutionary maps. A study of the latter would indicate that he drew from such experts as John

Mitchell, Lewis Evans and Thomas Hutchinson. But his was the first engraved in the United States by an American. His effort represents the driving spirit of a new republic. One can imagine the usefulness of this map during that hot summer of 1787.

To be sure, the delegates had large maps of their respective states, such as Henry Mouzon's map of North and South Carolina and their Indian Frontiers, printed in London in 1775, and the Fry and Jefferson map of Virginia and Maryland. But few citizens possessed these maps, and Buell was successful in making available to the general public a new map that combined all thirteen states.

Buell was born in Kilingworth, Connecticut in 1741. He got off to a raggedy start. In his youth he was apprenticed to a goldsmith, and thereafter he set himself up as a silversmith. He learned engraving, and to test his skills. he embarked upon raising a series of five shilling notes to a more comfortable denomination of five pounds, according to his biographer Lawrence Worth. For this error of judgement, he was tried, convicted, branded with the letter C on his forehead, imprisoned and his property confiscated. But after awhile the Connecticut Assembly released him from prison and restored his civil rights "from a compassionate regard and pity for his youthful follies." We don't know what they did about the C on his forehead, but presumably he carried it throughout his life. His two wives were testimony that it was not an encumbrance in the field of matrimony.

He next invented a lapidary machine for cutting and polishing precious stones.

He operated a line of packet boats between New Haven and New London. He learned type founding, and was loaned 100 pounds by the Connecticut Assembly to start a type foundry, but like many of his other projects, it ended in failure.

Later he developed a marble quarry, dabbled in privateering, cast type, practised the art of engraving, invented a machine for planting corn, and strangely enough secured permission to produce copper coins for the state of Connecticut, in spite of his record, after having invented a machine to do just that.

He has been described as restless, unstable, ambitious tinkerer, but nevertheless a practical genius. He died at the age of 81 in an alms house and was described in the newspapers' notice of his death as "an ingenious mechanic".

The map clearly delineates the large states with the vast territory they claimed to the west. Much of this land had been granted to particular colonies before the Revolution. Even after Yorktown and before the Treaty of Paris the various states were laying claim to it, and fussing amongst themselves. There was much confusion, especially in the region of the Northwest Territory. Of course Virginia claimed all of it, which was ignored by Massachusetts, Connecticut and Pennsyvlania. By 1787 the air was clearing, and a great portion of these Western lands had been ceded to the government by the various claiments. North Carolina granted much of what is now Tennessee to her war veterans in payment for their long service.

Abel Buell did the best he could under the circumstances, and errors contained therein are quaint, to say the least, and do not detract from his one enduring monument.

A.C.

New Jersey State Historical Society
Lawrence C. Wroth
American Heritage
Dictionary of American Biography